SHIFTING THINKING

The Entrepreneurs' Guide

To Exponential Growth

By CK Tan

 **RESULTS PRESS**

Results Press
Unit 229
#180, 8601 Lincoln Blvd.
Los Angeles, California
90045

www.theresultspress.com

ISBN: 978-1-953089-05-2

First Edition

Copyright © 2021 by CK Tan

All rights reserved. No part of this book may be reproduced in any form without the prior writer permission from the publisher. The opinions and conclusions drawn in this book are solely those of the author. The author and publisher bear no liability in connection with the use of the ideas presented.

Table of Contents

Chapter 1 Finding your purpose 11
   How your beliefs were formed 13
   Linking personality and purpose 14
   Your journey 17
   Values 19
   Reflection 22

Chapter 2 Being relevant is your mission 25
   Shifting demands 26
   Seeing the big picture 30
   Finding the right motivation 32
   Reflection 34

Chapter 3 Character 35
   Reflection 50

Chapter 4 Aligning your vision to your business 51
   A compelling vision for your business 51
   What problems can you solve? 54
   Seeing the end 56
   Reflection 58

Chapter 5 Leading in your business 59
   Leadership is about leading yourself 61
   Leadership is about serving others 63
   Leadership is about dreams and hopes 65
   Leadership is being proactive 66
   Leadership is about influence 67

Leadership is about confidence and having a winning attitude 68

Collaboration in leadership and in business 69

Reflection 70

Chapter 6 Overcome self-doubt and just do it 71

You are always connected 72

Fear that it won't go well 73

Not knowing where to start 74

Overcome self-doubt 76

Plan 77

Build capability 79

Take action 80

Take small, calculated steps 82

Where would you start? 83

Reflection 87

Chapter 7 Building results-based habits 89

Chapter 8 Harnessing your circle of influence 99

Why aren't you more influential? 103

Building powerful and high-trust relationships 104

Reflection 108

Chapter 9 Gaining breakthroughs in selling 109

Developing relationships to solve a problem 111

Developing the skills to solve a problem 114

Develop a consistent selling system 115

Develop a network of support 118

Develop a well-oiled automation process 119

Reflection 120

Chapter 10 Making impactful decisions 123

Your decision affects people around you 124

Passion affects your decisions 124

Your decision affects your business 125

Making decisions while looking at competing interests 126

Thinking in the moment 128

Decisions are based on emotions 129

Factors that influence the decision-making process for business owners and entrepreneurs 130

Reflection 131

Chapter 11 Impediments to success 133

Distractions 133

Procrastination 135

Taking charge of your success 139

Irrevocable decision 139

High-leverage activities 141

Reflection 141

Foreword

For nearly three decades I have shared the principles of high achievement and improved results—giving people the tools to live their lives and excel at business because they, and you, deserve more. I believe that it was intended that you live an abundant life. I've learned that it doesn't just happen; it isn't by chance. Your entire life is predicated on just two things—the decisions you make and the relationships you establish, nurture, and build. CK Tan is at the forefront of those professionals who are helping others achieve more and succeed at a higher level. Using proven strategies, CK shows up in a way that makes growth appear easy and change become the norm.

It doesn't matter where you come from or what you have or even haven't done—you have the ability to overcome any challenge and succeed beyond anything you may have ever thought possible. CK is an excellent example of this kind of persistence and perseverance. He has experienced his own challenges and become stronger as a result of overcoming those roadblocks. CK has utilized the lessons learned from these experiences to become the "go-to" for those entrepreneurs and high achievers who desire more than the hamster wheel that most of us have been taught to accept as the American Dream. CK chose to reject the generally accepted idea that he had to be satisfied with his life and made the decision to change. That decision was the pivot point, and it led him to a life of prosperity.

CK is a successful business owner who invests his time in helping others experience success and significance by guiding them to make the necessary changes in their lives and businesses. A highly sought-after mentor, consultant, and trainer, CK will give you the tools you need to achieve what you want and deserve, by sharing the steps that will enable you to make the changes that you need to make. Within these pages, you will learn what is holding you back and what you can do to ensure that you continue building the life and business that you know is possible. You will learn that you have the ability to expand and grow; to do those things that you never thought possible and have always known you could give yourself permission to execute.

Shifting Thinking will be a resource that you refer to repeatedly to help you discover and excavate your immense potential. Rarely do those things we perceive to be problems really turn out to be problems at all. We have falsely convinced ourselves that "it" just isn't possible. This book will allow you to explore the beliefs behind those thoughts and actions; it will give you all the tools you need to achieve the life and lifestyle that you want and deserve.

Shawn Shewchuk
The Productivity Speaker
The Number 1 Results Coach
2 X Bestselling Author
Movie Star

Chapter 1 Finding your purpose

Finding life's purpose is possibly one of the most challenging things that many people struggle with. It begs questions that sometimes take a lifetime to discover. Why are you here on this earth? For whom were you created? Many people leave this earth not knowing why they are here in the first place. It is the hyphen between your day of birth and your day of death that makes a person who he is and determines how he is remembered. I know many people, including me, who want to make a difference while living out the 'hyphen' but are not quite sure how to go about doing it. Or sometimes we are afraid of taking the steps required to make that difference.

Many years ago, my son asked me in one of our nightly devotions before bed, "Dad, you've always said that each of us has a purpose in life. What's yours?" I thought for a second, and it hit me. I have always told him that he will live out a great purpose in his life, but I did not take the time to reflect on why "I" was here. I seem to have the answers to my clients' problems but never really took the time to reflect on myself.

Since the time I was born, like many of you, my only purpose was to grow; to be potty-trained, to walk, and learn to be a good kid. Many of us spent at least 12 years in school and then in higher education, filling our minds with the way of the world, English,

Geography, Trigonometry, Calculus, Chemistry, Physics. Upon graduating from the formal educational years, we were then left on our own to survive—find a job, start a business, start a family. Our formative years in education left us with an abundance of knowledge of how the world operates, but it didn't teach us what our roles are.

Each of us has a purpose that continues to evolve, whether intentionally or otherwise. You may be a parent, a spouse, a child, a boss, an employee. You serve a purpose to different people that you are given the privilege to be with in your life. You may be the leader of a very successful company but, when you are home, your purpose becomes very different. My purpose as a business consultant is to help clients solve some of their biggest problems – with their organizations, strategies, people – and finally helping them with increasing their business growth and relevance in the marketplace. I am proud of the work that I deliver to my clients, and at times I feel like I have all the answers in the world.

When I am home, I am a spouse and a parent. How I lead myself impacts the decisions that I make in life. How I lead myself affects the choices that I make daily. These choices affect the actions that I take, and these actions are what define me—as an employer, a trusted advisor, a spouse, a son, a friend, and a parent.

As an entrepreneur, you have a business that is an expression of your personal goals and aspirations; it is an expression of your purpose. As your business grows, it becomes even more important for you as the leader to be more cognizant of the purpose of the business as it evolves, to make sure that it stays on track.

How your beliefs were formed

When my son was just about three years old, he saw me making wine from a wine kit, and he asked me, "Daddy, why are you spending so much time making wine? Why not just ask Jesus to turn water into wine? It's much faster". After several years of listening to a song with the line "water you turn into wine", at around age four, out of the unknown, he asked me that question. Well, that got me stuck. During the day, I can help multinational companies solve their problems, but I had no answers that evening when I was posed with that question. My answer to him that night, which probably wasn't the brightest answer, or even the correct one, was that "Jesus only does it at weddings". It was a turning point in my life when I realized that this little guy actually remembers what he hears and emulates the people he looks up to. He was influenced by what he heard and by my actions.

Believe it or not, the term 'monkey see, monkey do' applies to humans as well. From a very young age, babies try to imitate the adults around them, whether making funny noises or imitating and learning sign language. You may have also heard that 'imitation is the sincerest form of flattery'. Perhaps you have seen your friends wagging their tongues while playing basketball, in the hope that this action will stimulate them to perform like Michael Jordan.

As leaders, we are anchored in how our own beliefs are influenced by the people we look up to. Growing up, I did not see my mom very often. She was either out-of-town, coming home late from meetings, or attending evening schools. Many times, I would be the one to clean the house, make my own lunch and dinner and take care of things around the house. As I grew older, I understood how those experiences that I had growing up shaped my view on life and how my mom had such an influence on me growing up, although I did not see her that often or know that she was shaping me. Those years taught me to be independent, to finish up my schoolwork on time (with minimal supervision), to cook, to take care of life's basic necessities and to care for those around me. I would be lying to you if I said that I loved that life when I lived through it. It wasn't all pleasant. I would sometimes compare my mom with my friends; how their mom and dad were always there for them all the time.

My mom went to nursing school after high school. Upon getting her nursing diploma, she started a business instead of going into nursing. She literally built the business from the ground up amidst the challenges of an economic and political climate that wasn't favourable for her and her business. It became a successful business in the years that she led it. That wasn't enough for her, though. During that time, she went back to night school to get her diploma in business and eventually got an MBA. In the midst of that busyness of her life, she never failed to show her children the love that we needed (not the things that we wanted). I continuously strive to be like her as I now run my own business and have a family on my own.

Who in your life shapes who you are today? I understand that not everyone has someone in their immediate circle that they can look up to and emulate. Is there anyone in your life that influenced and shaped your purpose? If not, is there a public figure that you would like to 'be like'? Perhaps there are figures in your life that influenced you 'not to be like them'?

Linking personality and purpose

Countless books and literature have been produced to help us find that elusive answer to *What's my purpose?* Self-help books, personality tests, videos, daily devotionals, workshops and retreats have been designed and delivered to help you find just that. This is not a book about the 10 Steps of being a successful entrepreneur.

The purpose of this book is to offer you some guidelines with a few key steps that I believe will help you uncover some of your personality, purpose and potential towards having a successful business and life.

I was at a conference once and a speaker mentioned, "Think of the time when you were three or four years old. What did you like to do? What came to you naturally, before the world corrupted you"? It was a simple question that I had never thought of. That question, though simple, was deep. It has an element of truth in it. If you look at your children when they were at that age, they were (mostly) free to explore and discover the world around them.

My eldest son is quiet and reflective and Scrooge-like with his emotions, but he is a deep thinker, organized and detailed, while my younger son is more adventurous, open with his emotions, competitive, decisive and carefree. As I reflect, my behaviour when I was young was more like that of my eldest son. It would take a lot for me to interact with others I was not close to, whether friends or family. I could sometimes feel my parents' disappointment when I refused to play with the other kids or just hung out by myself in the corner. I've caught myself feeling dejected when my son, especially when he was younger, refused to give anyone any attention other than his immediate family.

My eldest son's behaviour is more aligned to mine when I was young. I recall that it took a lot for me to interact with others to whom I was not close. I could feel my parents' disappointment when I refused to interact with their friends or uncles and aunties with whom I did not have a close bond. Of course, I no longer dread interacting with people; in fact, it is what I do for a living now. But it is not something that comes naturally to me, and I have had to train myself in that.

However, as adults, we start using logic to discount some of these 'dreams' as time-wasters. "Stop dreaming", "Stop saying silly things", "What do you mean, when you travel to the sun?". As our kids grow up, some of these limiters become embedded into how we live our lives. Don't get me wrong—we need structures and rules to safely live in this world. Too much of it though, and we are at risk of losing what matters most—play time and discovery time. You might be wondering what that has to do with purpose? Well, your personality is crafted to fulfill a desire. If that personality becomes your identity and this identity satisfies your desire in life, that becomes your purpose. Many children today are told not to waste time and are sent to all kinds of activities after school; they will lack the ability to think independently and to dream.

Not many of us have the privilege of having all the stars lined up perfectly like that. For many of us, our purpose in life is what Daniel Pink states—that our purpose is a sense that we produce "something transcendent or serve something meaningful beyond ourselves".

These are the purposes that made the World Wide Web into a field of limitless knowledge and enabled sites such as Wikipedia to be the modern-day encyclopedia, where people would contribute information for little to no pay. There are many more sites where people freely share their expertise because it is that innate desire to contribute something transcendent and beyond themselves. These are the purposes that enabled techies to come together online to help you with your spreadsheet problems and share their knowledge with the world. For free! Need a solution for a problem? Just 'Google' it and countless answers are available for you to sift through. Pink argues that the theory of pay-for-performance is unsustainable because if they are motivated enough, people will do the work; sometimes with no pay!

Personalities are what define our outlook and how one operates. It's our DNA, so to speak. However, it doesn't mean that we stay there the rest of our lives. My intrinsic personality is that I am more inclined to be an introvert. But my purpose is to help business leaders and entrepreneurs see the success that they desire and deserve, and that fuels me to do what I do—many times with little to no pay. I would not be able to achieve what I want to achieve if I continued to be an introvert. My desire to see others succeed means that I need to rise above my intrinsic personality – to overcome my introversion – so that I am able to interact and be with clients and prospects. I am today what one might refer to as an 'ambivert', where I can be outgoing and enjoy spending time with others but still need my alone time to fuel up.

Your journey

Take a good hour for this exercise. Think of your own life journey and how you are shaped by it through your own life experiences. Divide your life into significant milestones. The ages are referenced as they are because these, I believe, are key pivot points in our lives, but feel free to alter them as they fit your key milestones.

- Childhood years (0 - 6 years)
    - Where were you born?
    - What were you like?
    - What were your key relationships?
    - How many siblings did you have, where did you fall in the sibling order?
    - What were the defining moments of your time— most difficult, important or unique?

- Elementary school years (6 - 12 years)
    - Where did you go to school?
    - What were you like?

- What were your key relationships?
- What were the defining moments of your time—most difficult, important or unique?

- Secondary/Middle/High School years (12 - 17)
  - Where did you go to school?
  - What were you like?
  - Who were your closest friends in school?
  - What were the defining moments of your time—most difficult, important or unique?

- College years (17 - 21 years)
  - Where did you go to college or university?
  - What were you like?
  - What were your key relationships?
  - What were the defining moments of your time—most difficult, important or unique?

- Early career (21 - 30)
  - Where was your first job? How long were you there?
  - What were you like as a young employee?
  - What were your key relationships?
  - What were the defining moments of your time—most difficult, important or unique?

- Mid to end career (30 - 50)
  - Where are you?
  - What is your role? What are you responsible for?
  - What are your key relationships?
  - What have been the defining moments of your time—most difficult, important or unique?
  - How did you become more creative in what you do?

- Mid to end career (50 - 75)
    - Where are you?
    - What is your role? What are you responsible for?
    - What are your key relationships?
    - How would you exit the professional world, and how would you like to be known?

As you reflect, what did you notice? What did you find interesting? Are there any themes or patterns that you see? How did these emerging themes shape you and the career path that you have chosen? How did your personality change? Who are the key influencers in your life? Do you see your purpose changing?

Values

Your values and beliefs direct your purpose and what you do while you are sojourning on this earth. In order to achieve your dreams, you need to start looking at your values. Your values are nothing but a set of behaviours that govern how you operate and how you arrive at the decisions that you make every day. Typically, for an entrepreneur, the values and operating principles of a business mirror each other. They are the cornerstone of your idea. In a typical workplace, if the values of an organization align with the values of the individual or team, you can bet your bottom dollar that the employees are happy and will go above and beyond at work.

These could include keywords such as 'Accountability', 'Ambitious', 'Faith', 'Family', 'Generosity', 'Perfection', 'Trustworthiness' and so on.

A business's operating principles, or values, typically will not change overnight, but they must be looked at frequently to ensure that they continue to be relevant and lived by. Over the years of advising organizations and businesses, I have seen companies and businesses debate over what their vision, mission and values are, and how they continue to shift as market demands.

When I facilitate Priority Management's WorkingSm@rt programs, one of the things that participants have to think about is creating a link from their everyday to-dos and tasks to a bigger picture and what is referred to as values-based productivity. Participants have a chance to evaluate their values and note what is important for them. What is important for them is derived from their belief system. Our belief system is usually formed from a combination of our upbringing, our culture, our life experiences, and our intrinsic personality. Over time, the reinforcement of these elements ultimately becomes our values.

Values may alter as we evolve and when our circumstances change. Your values will change over time as well. But your core values – the basis of your being – should remain consistent. If you were to add your values to those 'life intervals' exercises that you just completed, what would they be, and did they change over the course of your life?

According to Patrick Lencioni in his book *The Advantage*, values can be put into several categories. Two of these are 'Accidental' values and 'Aspirational' values. Accidental values are traits that we demonstrate unintentionally. These values are typically derived from our culture and upbringing. Aspirational values, on the other hand, are simply characteristics that we see our future self having; something that we strive for and work towards becoming.

Aspirational values are what drive us forward. Our aspirational values may also change as circumstances evolve. I am writing this book in the middle of the COVID-19 pandemic that has seen the world change overnight. At the time of school closures in the middle of March 2020, I still had plans to have my two children bussed to school until the very last day, but by the first two days of the school closure announcement, my sons were the only kids in their classrooms. My priorities had to change to accommodate that. The way I work, and the way many of us approached work, had changed literally overnight. Some of these changes will be long-term. The structure in which our lives are shaped have shifted dramatically. Work life integration became more real than ever. This is important because as entrepreneurs and small business owners, work and life are tightly integrated. Part of the business purpose lines up with life's purpose. COVID-19 became a pivot point for many people, and I include myself in that. I had to rethink how I deliver services to my clients, what it is that clients are looking for and how they can embrace the change that is happening to their businesses and their lives. People who had not thought of starting a business began to see this as an opportunity to live out a dream that had been buried deep down in exchange for job security. People who had businesses had to think of ways to continue being relevant in the new world. At the beginning stages of the pandemic, I reached out to clients, associates, and businesses that I work with, and just in the city alone, 90% of businesses were re-evaluating their strategies to adapt to a new future—a future that no one had predicted in February 2020 and one that is likely to become permanent in many ways, shapes and forms.

Sometimes, on the journey towards an aspirational value, you might have to reboot. The reboot process might very well be demanding and challenging. You will have to change your paradigm and shift your mindset. It is easier said than done. It's all about getting out of your comfort zone.

Reflection

Here is a quick exercise that will help you find out what your core values are.

First, take some time to list 10 of your cherished values. Your values dictate how you behave and how you arrive at decisions in life.

Here are some thought starters on some keywords that may resonate with you as you work through your own core values:

Loyal	Resourceful
Responsive	Faithful
Continuous learning	Fun
Service	Success-oriented
Integrity	Honest
Respect	Courageous
Loving	Excited
Committed	Orderly
Dependable	Collaborate
Adventurous	Creative
	Efficient

These are simply examples. If this list does not include some of the things that you value, feel free to add them to your own list. There are no right or wrong answers to these.

1.
2.

3.
4.
5.
6.
7.
8.
9.
10.

These values make up what you are. Rank the top three of these values based on their importance to you and your life. These are typically the values that are true for you—those that you would never second guess, no matter what you are doing. If your top value is being 'loyal', there is no way in hell I can make you betray someone, even if it means sacrificing yourself just so you remain true to that value.

1.
2.
3.

Now think of your average day. How are you living your values every day? How much time do you devote to building and living out the values that you have listed? Do you stop for a few minutes at the end of every day to evaluate yourself on how your day was? What you did well today, what did not go so well that needs for you to redirect so that you're ready for tomorrow? Continuing to do this every day will definitely be a way that you live up to who you are created to be. Many people do not spend nearly enough time sharpening themselves. A quote that I recently heard was "A dead fish can swim downstream". Are you swimming downstream and living your life by default, or are you intentional about living out your values every day, even if it seems challenging?

A business also has values. For an entrepreneur, the values of the business owner are closely tied to the values of the business. Similarly, the values or operating principles of an organization will consist of some core values (values that will not change) and some aspirational values. Sometimes these values may alter slightly, as the organization evolves and in response to market forces.

Chapter 2 Being relevant is your mission

"I will build a car for the great multitude. If I had asked people what they wanted, they would have said faster horses" - Henry Ford

"If we worked on the assumption that what is accepted as true really is true, then there would be little hope for advance" - Orville Wright

"A computer on every desk, and in every home, running Microsoft software" - Bill Gates

"An iPod, a phone, an internet mobile communicator. These are not three separate devices! We are calling it iPhone. Today Apple is going to reinvent the phone" - Steve Jobs

"You're changing the way cities work, and that's fundamentally a third rail. We're in a political campaign, and the candidate is Uber and the opponent is named Taxi" - Travis Kalanick

What if the people who made these quotes believed that what they said bordered on ridiculousness? These ideas came from people who dared to dream. More important than their ideas is that they had laser focus and bull-headed persistence, and that turned their dreams into reality. To be clear, some of these were not original ideas, but with relentless pursuit and hard work, these men looked at what is and, instead of accepting the status quo, asked "Why not?", seized the opportunity, innovated existing ideas, and changed humanity.

Dreams change worlds. Dreams revolutionize humanity. Unfortunately, since the beginning of the industrial revolution about a hundred years ago and the creation of the assembly line, we have been trained to conform. Schools teach us to fit into a box, fit into a convention, don't rock the boat. We are trained to study well so that when we graduate, we will get a secure job, be a good worker for the next 30 years and leave with a gold watch and a farewell cake. We become do-ers of things, not thinkers. The world continuously pushes for mass production, lower cost, economies of scale to support consumerism so we can purchase things at lower prices. What better way to create economies of scale than to train humans to conform to a specific behaviour?

Challenge yourself. Look at the world around you. What else can be done to make life better? What problems are you trying to solve? I am not talking about grandiose and impossible dreams (or am I?) to promote world peace and save the turtles. I'm talking about dreams that you can make sense of. These dreams start with having the right set of values. Refer to the previous chapter and review the values that you have listed. How aspirational are they? Do your aspirational values make you uncomfortable? If they do, that's the first step towards making your dream a reality. But you may ask, "Where do I start?" Whether you are an entrepreneur or a loyal employee, you can be a force for change and change for the better.

Shifting demands

Since this book is written during the health pandemic of 2020 and 2021, let's look at this as a market force. Businesses that stubbornly maintain that the people will come back, and we do not have to change the way the business works, unfortunately, will be, and are, left behind. I had the opportunity to work with several businesses during the pandemic, to shift their focus and finding alternative ways to reach their clients. One was a business that did not believe in the effectiveness of online marketing but was ultimately forced to embrace the idea because that was likely the only available channel to reach their customers. To their surprise, several days after they went live, they had inquiries from people from other countries! These were customers that they otherwise would not have the ability to connect with. Those who can pivot their business to meet market demands will always have an edge over those who continue to maintain the status quo. Think about big companies that were very successful in the past, such as Sears Roebuck Company, Blackberry, Toys 'R Us, and JC Penney, which had to close hundreds of stores worldwide, exit entire markets, and exit entire product lines because they did not keep up or understand the changing nature of their clientele.

Some of these companies successfully pivoted their business model to meet changing demands. Think of the following companies:

- Blackberry (or Research In Motion, as it was corporately known when the company first started) created the smartphone market, and at its peak it controlled over 50 percent of the smartphone market globally. By failing to read consumer taste and evolution, especially with the release of full-touch screen phones, its market share dropped to a negligible number when compared to the global smartphone makers. Today, Blackberry no longer makes smartphones and focuses its attention on what it's always been synonymous with − security − and today it is recognized as a big force in cyber security.
- IBM, a company now known as one of the early pioneers of the computer and operating systems, started out as "International Business Machines". After a few missteps in

the 1990s and early 2000s, it is now a fully service-oriented firm.

- General Electric was once a major player in appliances but has now transformed itself into a global conglomerate of many businesses in various industries, none of which involve household appliances (although there are still GE-branded appliances, it is now majority owned by Haier and marketed as GE Appliances).

You may not be able to associate with some of these case studies, but you might recognize that some of your local distilleries and breweries retooled their operations to produce hand sanitizers in a matter of weeks—that's an example of pivoting a business to meet market demands. By doing so, these distilleries not only met an immediate market need but were able to help solve the huge problem of a shortage of hand sanitizer.

Retooling a distillery to produce hand sanitizer is not an overly complicated process. It just requires a re-blending of chemicals to ensure that the alcohol produced is not drinkable. Typically, it is the retooling of the distillery to revert to producing beverages and spirits that would require additional capital investment, because the hoses and pumps that were filled with the additional chemical cannot easily be removed.

Adam Sperling, the President of the Prairie Craft Spirits Association, received calls from first responders, including hospitals, municipalities, law enforcement and mobile medical units, asking for disinfectant because there was a global shortage exacerbated by the disruption of logistics in the supply chain in the middle of March 2020, when the lockdown was announced. Adam, in concert with the association, responded to the need quickly by donating pure alcohol at no charge to any first responders that required it. He also facilitated the retooling of some of its member distillers to produce hand sanitizers, while communicating and facilitating the regulatory process across multiple levels of government to quicken the licensing process that includes inspections, permitting, alignment of recipes with the federal guidelines, and other related regulations. This is a process that would have normally taken at least six months, but it was reduced to a matter of days and weeks. Supply throughout the Province of Saskatchewan was quickly met; one reason for the quick turnaround was that the province is one of the largest global suppliers of grain-derived alcohol used in many industrial, pharmaceutical, personal care, flavour, fragrance and beverage brands.

Restaurants and supermarkets became creative in how they reached their customers. Services such as no-contact pick-ups and drop-offs became the norm rather than channels to reach customers. Virtual meetings became the norm instead of group conferences or meetings in a coffee shop. Products such as Microsoft Teams, Zoom, GoTo and Slack exploded and, at one point, could not keep up with the exponential demands of users from all over the world. These products and services were forced to innovate to be top-of-mind for their customers.

In a short two-month period, the amount of innovation that took place in many businesses, big or small, was astronomical!

It didn't just stop there. As the recovery progressed and conferences started to be held again, another set of entrepreneurs emerged. Once again, a need was recognized—this time on COVID-19 testing for travelers. These entrepreneurs struck deals that allowed labs to go to conference sites (usually hotels and conference centres) and provide on-site testing. Conference attendees did not need take a cab ride to a testing centre and wait in line, or pay astronomical fees for testing at the airport. The profit margin was very good, and they sold their services on convenience.

Remember, the bigger the problem you can solve, the bigger your value is in the eyes of your customers. Do you know of any businesses in your area that went out of their way to stay ahead of the curve and to fulfill the demands of the market?

Seeing the big picture

What's the point of all these stories? It's all about where you think you want to go and how you will get there. In that journey, there will be challenges and difficulties, and it is all about how prepared you are to navigate yourself and your business across the desert. Think of your end product as a fully grown plant and imagine yourself as the seed. If you left a seed on its own, it is dormant and unable to do anything. To be able to accomplish anything, you need to start by being buried in soil and fertilized, possibly by manure. I can imagine it not being too comfortable, and it probably wouldn't smell very nice either! While you are in the cold, uncomfortable place, you will start to grow roots and become stronger. Once the roots take hold, you will begin to emerge from the soil. That's your first breakthrough. As you continue to grow, your roots become stronger, and in a short time, you will be a fully grown plant. This is the second habit from Stephen Covey—begin with the end in mind. The Israelites had to sojourn in the desert for 40 years before they could arrive at the promised land because they needed to be shaped up.

It's great to read copious amounts of leadership and business books. It's great to participate in workshops and feel-good seminars to gain the knowledge that you require to grow. More importantly, though, it's about what you *do* with that knowledge. Having just head knowledge is not going to get you the results you desire. Success depends on the number of high-leverage activities that you do. Every day. Sometimes, that also means getting some road rash along the way.

To know where you want to go, you need to start reflecting on your current reality and look at how determined you are to want to go where you want to go.

First off, examine your current reality and start with your level of satisfaction in yourself. Take a hard look at your life in the last 7 days. Are you able to list the high-leverage activities that you have done? If you just look at your day yesterday and dissect the hours to an average of eight hours, how many of those hours did you spend building yourself up and building your business? Normally, we like to justify that we are busy. But what are you busy with? Are you busy with things that will give you the best bang for the buck, or are you just busy doing stuff that adds no value to yourself or your business?

Reflect on your day yesterday and fill this table out. This is your reality.

Time intervals	What I did	Should I be doing this?	What I should do instead
8am–10am			
10am–12pm			
12pm–1pm			
1pm–3pm			
3pm–5pm			

Are you happy with what you have written down?

The time intervals are just an indication for you. If you start your day at 6am, go ahead and change the headings. The whole purpose of this is for you to take stock of your life. Are you making the most of it? Remember, the results that you want are directly correlated to the activities that you do to achieve them.

Building off of the values exercise that you did in the previous chapter, how much time do you devote to building on the values that are aspirational to you? Where do you see the gaps? One of the first things that I encourage in clients I coach is to continue pushing themselves further every day. Towards the end of the day, they are to journal their day and evaluate themselves based on goals they have set daily It is not an exercise to beat yourself down, but to be honest with yourself that, since you have committed to bettering your life, you must take the steps necessary to challenge your status quo and be better.

Finding the right motivation

Much has been written about motivation, and there are many theories about how to get people motivated. There is also the concept of intrinsic and extrinsic motivation. Extrinsic motivation means that we do what we do in order to 'gain something'. That something could be recognition, a sense of belonging, a trophy, or any type of external reward that will push us forward to continue doing that activity. Extrinsic motivation can also come in a negative form, where you would be punished or reprimanded if you do not achieve something. This is the carrot-and-stick argument of motivation. The real world that we live in is filled with extrinsic motivation. We go from one 'motivation' to the next 'motivation'. We want a new device every year because it makes us feel good, to hold the next shiny thing until the next shiny thing comes along. Or maybe it's to belong, so we are able to show our friends that we have the latest and greatest gadget. Security updates and obsolescence aside, we want these new devices because it makes us feel good. At work, we want to be recognized as the person that was the top performer because it comes with more pay increases. These are all external motivators that act as the 'carrot' in the carrot-and-stick model.

If you are an entrepreneur and business owner, you will quickly realize that external motivators are not sustainable, especially when you are just in the beginning stages of building your business. You need to be driven by an intrinsic need and belief that what you do is something significant. Take the Internet, for example. If you need to know how to perform a specific spreadsheet function, more likely than not you will find that information somewhere on the Internet. Much of the information on the Internet is provided and shared by people who were willing to share their knowledge. For free. That is why the concept of pay-for-performance is now considered outdated and has been replaced by other methods of motivation that speak to intrinsic motivators of the individuals. This is not an easy task for many, especially when it comes time to find that true motivator and what it looks like. It takes a lot of self-realization, patience and speaking truthfully to yourself.

Reflection

To do this exercise, wake up an hour earlier and before everyone else.

1. From the time tracking table that you completed, rate your accomplishments of yesterday. How did you think you do? Why did you rate yourself the way you did? What would it take for you to move the score higher?

2. Think of your business and your passion—what is it that really drives you to perform and to do what you do, where you would spend many hours perfecting your craft because you are so passionately tied to it? What is it that wakes you up on a Monday morning and have you screaming "Happy Monday" and that you're glad you 'get to do this'?

3. Maybe you are in a job today but dread going to work every day. You may be doing it because "the money is good" or "I'm doing my time for another two years before I retire". If these were not limiting factors, what would you be doing instead, and where will you find fulfillment? What's stopping you?

Chapter 3 Character

Let each one test his own work, and then his reason to boast will be in himself alone and not in his neighbour.

—Paul's letter to the Galatians (6:4)

Values are like a compass with which our actions and behaviour are guided. These guiding principles and standards are what we deem as the right way when we conduct ourselves and especially when we are faced with a difficult challenge or a conflict. Values then become the variable by which we make choices.

One of my favourite and easiest ways to explain values is through the Competing Values Framework that was developed by Robert Quinn and Kim Cameron.

This model has been in existence for over 30 years and continues to be relevant to individuals and businesses. The authors suggest that individuals and organizations typically fall into one of the four 'dominant' quadrants that define them.

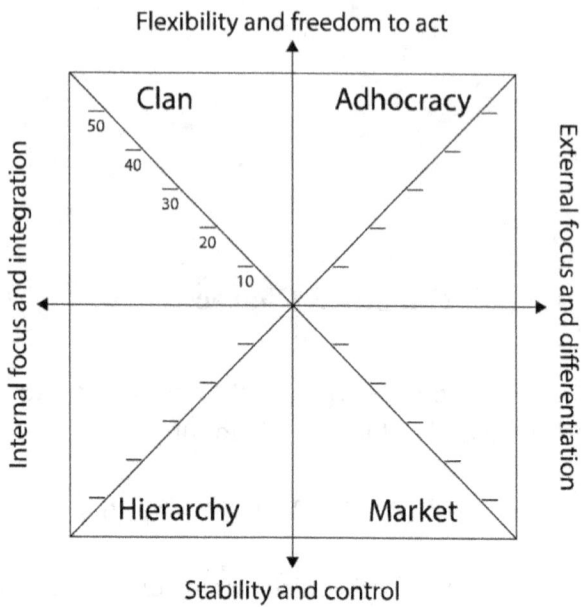

This model has been in existence for over 30 years and continues to be relevant to individuals and businesses. The authors suggest that individuals and organizations typically fall into one of the four 'dominant' quadrants that define them. For example, if you are a collaborator, you are possibly a longer-term person versus a person who is looking for short-term gains and wants to do things fast. If you are a person who is in control and wants to do things right, you will have a competing value that is more ad-hoc, or creative. There are no right or wrong answers to the assessment—it is a snapshot of your own values and how they compete with each other.

Character, on the other hand, is more outward. It is a person's attributes or features, which are visible and distinct to an individual. When we are consistent in behaving or acting in a certain way, it forms character.

Just as with values, sometimes we need to build our character up to be able to achieve the vision that we set for ourselves. It is hard work; this won't be easy. You have heard of the adage that it takes 21 days to form a habit (some studies have shown it would take several months). But regardless of the number of days, it is about our intention to build good character.

There have been times when I was caught not doing 'excellent work' when I was supposed to be. While I should be doing high-leverage activities (such as writing this book) or contacting clients or prospects, I sometimes catch myself browsing the web (and spending too much valuable time on it). When one of my boys came over to ask what I was doing, he caught me not doing excellence. When you find yourself feeling a slight 'guilt', you can be sure that you're probably not doing the right tasks. Sometimes accountability from an 8-year-old is enough to give you a kick-in-the-rear-end to start doing things right and doing them well.

From my years as an entrepreneur, working with and training clients, and operating businesses, there were a few characteristics that I find really define an entrepreneur and business owner. It is important, as you embark on your entrepreneurial career, that these are essential characteristics that you have or continue to build up as you move along in the journey.

1. Passion

    Nothing can be more straightforward than being passionate about what you do. It is the quintessential characteristic of a business owner and being an entrepreneur. It is so common to hear of people who wake up every Monday, count the days until Friday and repeat the same process week after week for years, just to collect the pension that awaits them at the end of their service. Passion is the fuel that keeps the entrepreneur going even when things are tough and when you're not seeing the returns that you expect when you expect to see them. Passion will somehow present itself when you are in a crowd or when you are promoting your business. It is infectious, and you can see it through someone who is passionate about what they do.

Let's look at someone that we all (at least many people) know—Bill Gates. To the regular person, he does not seem like an exciting guy if you were to compare him to Steve Jobs. But you can definitely feel Bill Gates' passion when he goes on to talk about what he has invented. Though not as polished a presenter as Steve Jobs, when he starts talking about computers and software, you can definitely see his passion shine through his eyes. He mentioned in an interview that he only takes a week off work in a year (this was in the early 1990s) and guess what—he takes that week to read Ph.D dissertations on computers and technology! Talk about passion!

You have an idea that you'd like to sell, whether it is a training course, a candle, a painting, a piece of music, your delicious cooking, or a process that you have spent time developing. Think about how passionate you were when you thought of the idea. When you are asked about it, do you suddenly find yourself elevated and able to talk about it without any script? That's your passion.

2. Excellence

Having an excellent character and delivering excellence is paramount to being an entrepreneur. It is all about going above and beyond and delighting the customer, which will set you apart as a business owner.

How many times have you seen 'Excellence' as a key trait of a business, only to find that people who are working there do not feel like they want to be there? We see that all the time, everywhere and in many businesses. This is when there is no alignment between the workers and the business owner.

One of my favourite quotes was one that I saw in a viral video by Rick Rigsby entitled "Lessons from a Third Grade Dropout", where he quoted his dad, a third-grade dropout, as saying, "One of these days my boys will catch me in an act of excellence". What a profound quote. That shows a character of excellence. What caught my attention was that excellence is repeated conduct that one is aware of at all times. We should be doing the right things, and doing things right and doing things well, even when no one is watching.

As a business partner, I make myself available at all times to my clients as they need me; I know that in some of their businesses they might need me at odd hours of the day or week. Of course, this is within reason, and we set the ground rules early in the engagement that there may be times that I might not be available because family comes first for me, especially when I am on family time. When I am with my client, I make sure that *they* are my one concern; that they are the most important person in the room. My phones are turned to silent, and the client has my full attention. I will spend the time necessary, even if it takes long hours to come up with solutions with them as they need. This is my way of showing excellence, both at home and at work.

3. Ambition

    You cannot be a successful entrepreneur if you are not ambitious. If you are not ambitious, you could just go out and find a stable job and be content with what you've got. There's nothing wrong with that. To be successful at your career and take it to new heights, or to build a business, it takes a different kind of ambition and courage to reach those goals.

    Where do you see yourself in 24 months? If you are reading this book now and re-read it in 24 months, what will have been different in your life and your business? Have you achieved the goals that you have set for yourself today?

    Remember, your ambition shapes the performance of your business and your ventures, and it is where your vision sets in. From your vision come your plans and actions. Without an ambitious end goal, you will likely not achieve what you set out to achieve. This is where the famous adage comes in (paraphrased)—aiming for the moon and hitting a few stars along the way is better than aiming at the tree in your backyard and hitting it all the time.

4. Diligence

    We live in an 'instant generation'—instant noodles, instant information, instant communication, instant gratification. Investors are looking for instant or short-term gains. If you have started a business before, you know that the word 'instant' is probably not in your vocabulary. It takes time and it takes work—lots of hard work. Ask the local restaurant owner how many hours he spends at his 'office'. It's definitely not 9-5 from Monday to Friday.

This is especially true during a business's infancy. It takes time to plan, to oversee, and to execute. Depending on the amount of available funds and the resources you have, you may need to be on ground level, handing out flyers, performing the actual work that you sell, and more.

When I started out in business, there were things that I did not know that came with the package of launching on your own. Apart from the passion that I have for helping people see success, I needed to let people know what I do. This comes from reaching out to people, attending networking events, posting on social media, having a website and keeping it updated, tracking the sales process, measuring clients' (and my own) business results, doing the actual work, managing taxes, working out budgets and finances, managing employees (the worst is when they don't show up for work and you have a client waiting to be served!), and, most importantly, to still make time for the family. There were definitely areas that I was good at, and many that I was not good at. These were the areas that I needed the most help with. Like many startups, I started doing everything on my own until I got myself into trouble for not knowing what I didn't know—more on that in Chapter 9 where I write about building a team.

It is something that you need to be mentally prepared for, and your family needs to be alongside you as you walk this journey. It will take up a lot of your time, and it will take a lot out of you, but like many business owners that I have spoken to, it is worth all the effort.

Michael Gerber, in his book *E-Myth*, describes it perfectly. The founder of a business needs to read across three personalities—the entrepreneur (the visionary and dreamer), the manager (the pragmatic planner) and the technician (the do-er).

Many people want to start a business because they are good and passionate about something. That's an excellent start. The problem comes when the business does not sell as much as was hoped for or there's a lack of discipline in the execution of the business plan to keep the business running and thriving. That's when administrative and leadership skills need to be accompanied by working smart and working hard. I have known a few very talented chefs who wanted to own their own restaurants. Great intentions. These same chefs would not hesitate or think twice about putting in the newest and shiniest kitchen equipment and tools, but they lack the knowledge for actually running and building a business. Many of these restaurants end up being closed because of bad investment decisions and money management, as well as insufficient processes when it comes to planning and implementing a business strategy.

5. Grit

"You're climbing a mountain, you got your mountain climber shoes on. You gotta get those knees up if you're gonna make it to the top!"

— Shaun T (Beachbody trainer)

The strength of your mind determines your perseverance and your grit. Mattie Ross, a character in Charles Portis' novel *True Grit*, is a 14-year-old girl on a quest to avenge her father's death by capturing his alleged murderer, in spite of the adversities and challenges that faced women in the late 19th century, let alone a 14-year-old girl. Mattie displayed true courage and perseverance in breaking down barriers and pushing through setbacks to achieve her aim of capturing the murderer, ultimately losing an arm in the journey to reach her goal.

Perseverance also means you need to sometimes get out of your comfort zone. I am naturally an introvert; I don't typically like to be out there meeting new people or being in social events with people I don't know on a personal level. I had to train myself to shift my thinking to "People need my services, and it is a responsibility that I be out there to seek out people that would need my support" and "I can't be selfish".

For a business owner, things will not go smoothly. But it's how you respond to the adversities that will determine your level of motivation to keep going on when you are faced with failure and struggle.

6. Decisiveness

"When can I start my business", "Should I wait until all the stars align before I get started"?

There's no better time than now. There's no better time than when you are ready for it. Of course, I caveat that with the analysis that you need to make sure that you have the right product or service in the right market at the right price point. But do it. Do it imperfectly and start progressing. As an entrepreneur, you cannot afford to be indecisive. Yes, there will be times when you take a bit longer to analyze a situation, but after all is said and done, you need to decide. Being proactive is a key characteristic of a decisive entrepreneur.

In the midst of uncertainties surrounding the hospitality and restaurant industry, Sergio made the decision to open a restaurant. When I asked him why in mid-2020, when the restaurant industry was one of the hardest hit. His answer was one of confidence: "Why not now?"

It's been two years since Sergio started his first restaurant. Since then, he has also opened up Agave Authentic Mexican Grill, a very well-received – and possibly the best – Mexican restaurant in the Canadian prairies! To overcome the supply problems plaguing many business owners, Sergio sought to partner with local producers and suppliers. He is also a big believer in giving back to the community. Once, when a local supplier gifted him with potatoes, he turned them into potato cream soup and gave it away, for free!

Sergio has this to say: "No regrets". Be decisive like Sergio and don't look back. Learn along the way.

Not all decisions are cut and dried; sometimes you must choose between two imperfect options. I had one long-term employee that was toxic to the business and was causing trouble on the premises with a negative attitude and a tendency to gossip and talk back, making others in the team feel like being at work every day was a chore. At the same time, I didn't know if I could afford to let this employee go because he was generating sales and had a few customers that would follow him closely. Eventually, I had to decide between bottom-line sales and having a better work culture at the office. After I made a decisive and swift action to cut ties with him, the camaraderie at the office changed almost overnight, and overall sales improved!

Being decisive sometimes means you need to always see the opportunity instead of the calamity. For example, should I spend $1,000 monthly on advertising? For the person that sees the opportunity, it is about investing $1,000 to potentially receive $3,000 in additional revenue, but for the person who sees it as another expenditure, you will lose $1,000 instead of gaining the $3,000. It is all a matter of perspective and taking proactive measures.

Sometimes, opportunities may come your way as an entrepreneur, and you must decide whether they are in line with what you believe in. I have friends who come up to me and ask if I was willing to be in their MLM (Multi-Level Marketing, or Network Marketing) team because they believe the products that they offer are very much aligned with what I do or there are opportunities to invest in projects that are also 'in line' with what I do. These are some things that will present themselves, and you must quickly decide in your heart where you would like to see your business going. You want to have a niche, and you do not want to be spread out and be known as everything to everyone you see. This is where decisiveness comes in. Be clear on what you do and what you offer; have the courage to say "no" if an opportunity comes your way and you do not think it fits nicely into your vision.

7. Resourcefulness

At the peak of the economic challenges that accompanied the COVID pandemic, the perseverance of several business owners that I know shone through in the face of adversity. A business owner who ran a garden in the outskirts of a city found himself needing to reach clients in a different way. Within weeks, he set up his online store, reaching out to clients through a daily Facebook live event, showcasing the little farm animals that he has and the products that are available for sale (by delivery or contactless pickup). That's just one example of many who had followed a similar course of action.

A church in town, instead of responding negatively to the shutdowns and the lack of the ability to congregate, had instead reached out to the community in kind by visiting their congregants and offering baskets of gifts to those in need, singing at the care homes, and offering their sanctuary to be a place the authorities could use for any reason.

At times, being resourceful is also not being afraid to ask for help. Several years ago, to help in a project, I put together a team of professionals from across the country that had never worked together. We won the project and executed the engagement successfully, and even today this team continues to lean on each other for help in other ways, years after the project was completed. Many of my initiatives and projects are based on that model, and it has proven to be successful in more ways than one.

How flexible are you in your business? Do you have the ability to scale your business, both upwards and downward, as required? Do you live in the scarcity mindset that what you have is all you have, or are you flexible enough to think outside the box to see the possibilities that could present themselves? These are questions that you need to ask yourself in your business as you begin to look at your resources and what you can accomplish.

8. Risk Taker

The fact that you are reading this book (if I did not force it on to you) is enough to make you start thinking of what's possible. If you are already a business owner, you know that you already are taking a risk. You are abandoning the steady paycheque, a structured life, a steady cash flow, and a stable job (that's debatable today) for something that is totally unpredictable and could mean sacrificing a lot of things that you take for granted.

Being an entrepreneur and taking risks are tied in together. There isn't one without the other. Starting a business means either taking a chunk of your own savings or getting a large loan (or a combination of both) and embarking on an unknown adventure. You may also be an unknown character in the field that you are venturing into.

I took a risk by letting that employee go, but I had to if I wanted to keep the rest of the team. I calculated that the risk of keeping that employee was higher than if I let him go. I took a risk, too, when I invested in the marketing strategy, because it might not go as well as I planned it to. We can do the risk analysis like an actuarial scientist, or we could go with the gut feel.

Do you see the glass as half-empty or half-full when you are making the decision to take the risk of executing a plan? To be clear, not all of your risks will pay off. Some will, and some won't. How good are you with walking away when something doesn't work the way you had planned it? Do you have a risk management plan that will tell you when the 'cut-off' is? Just like a smart investor or gambler, know your limits and what you're able to handle.

9. Good Listener

I can't stress this enough. Being an entrepreneur also means you need to listen. Listening is an important characteristic that you need to demonstrate as a business owner. It's not just listening to your prospective clients. It also means listening to your employees, to your business associates, to your family, and to yourself!

I sometimes fall into the trap of telling about all the good things I must sell without first listening to what my clients need. It takes skill to sit back and just take the time and the energy to listen and understand before we can add value. Business is about building relationships and solving problems for each other.

By March 2020, we could not hold group training sessions because of the pandemic. We quickly found ways to connect with our clients because we knew they were having trouble collaborating with their team virtually, and leaders did not have the required skills to lead from home. Our clients came to us for help. Instead of selling them the 'virtual' sessions of the training that we already have, we asked ourselves, "What are the actual problems that our clients are seeing today?" They were stressed out and did not have the proper skills to manage and work remotely when family, life, career and school integrated into a form that no one could see coming. Priority Management International, over the course of a few weeks, developed a workshop that was geared towards working smart from the home and how to work smart as a remote leader. That supported millions of people across the world to develop a better strategy for working and leading a team virtually.

Information is available about anything and everything but do your own research to separate fact from fiction. Read peer-reviewed publications and find out what the market is looking for. Listen also to the world around and the evolution that is going on. Listen to your competitors, innovators and thought leaders. Read their whitepapers, explore their websites, run market surveys and stay ahead of the curve.

As a business owner, the one thing that you should not neglect is yourself and your family. We tend to overwork to keep the business running or growing, so that we forsake what matters most. Employees come and go and clients come and go, but it's our family and our body that will be there for us through thick and thin. Make sure that the family is aware of everything that you are doing; pull them along for the ride and listen to what they need as well.

10. Giver

Many business owners may already know this, but it is so important that we give and contribute to society in more ways than one. At the start of my business, I was giving free coaching, training and advice to people who needed it. There were two reasons for this: I was passionate about what I do, and I was willing to share the information I have. As well, I needed to create awareness of the services that I was selling. By giving out free information and access to my services, I was able to promote myself. Similarly, you may see some establishments giving out free samples to try. This is one way of giving to receive more.

Giving also does not need to have an ulterior motive. If you are passionate about what you do and are motivated by it, there is no need to force yourself to give and to contribute. Giving yourself, both financially and in time dedicated to causes that you care about, is an important characteristic of a successful entrepreneur. You may be giving to your local church or to a charity that you deeply care about, and you serve those with your time and finances to the best of your ability.

In my case, making money is important but I am also guided by the verse, "The love of money is the root of all evil". The money that I make enables me to contribute to things that I am passionate about—sponsoring a child on World Vision, giving to community organizations, and partnering with a not-for-profit organization. It provides me with the freedom to choose what I do with my time and money to make a difference in my community.

Reflection

1. Have you ever been caught doing an 'excellent work'? What was it? Who caught you? How did it make you feel?

2. Number the ten characteristics in order from the one that you most identify with and fit the best to the one you find most challenging. What will you do to move the needle on the difficult characteristics you need to improve on?

Chapter 4 Aligning your vision to your business

In the last three chapters, we were focused on you – the individual, the entrepreneur – and how you are able to identify and develop a sense of purpose; how your values determine your behaviour and the actions that you take.

As an entrepreneur, it is common for your business to become your life. If you currently have a business, you will be able to relate to some of the common misconceptions that the general public has about the business owner.

"You have your own business? Must be great being your own boss."
"You must be able to go on vacation anytime you want."
"Must be nice working for yourself—no boss barking down at you."

These phrases might be commonly heard about people in business. For anyone who has ever started a business, this is probably far from reality, at least until the business is fully established and can run on its own!

A compelling vision for your business

Many entrepreneurs do not spend the time to look at what their business is about. Most, particularly if they are into consulting or coaching, would want to be everything to everybody to get all the business they can get. Although it's a good way of staying afloat and keeping your lights on, particularly in the early days of a business, it is not sustainable long term.

In the early years of my business, I was working on every little thing that I could get my hands on to keep me going. I dabbled in the insurance industry and multi-level marketing, and I volunteered my skillsets by helping other entrepreneurs with their business ventures. I bought a couple of businesses and operated them; I became a facilitator, trainer and owner of another business, and I also led various consulting projects and business ventures. On top of that, I volunteered in many different community organizations and political events. I was all over the place, and I lacked focus and direction—not knowing where I was heading. After a few years of diving into all kinds of activities, I was a jack-of-all-trades; I knew everything but didn't know anything. I decided that I needed to focus.

Fast forward a few years later. I told myself that this is not sustainable, and I needed to be more single-minded on something that will stir me up. It is important to make money, but it is even more important that I get into something that I am good at, that I can add exceptional value to those I work with and to make a difference. Many people can take that epiphany and can focus their attention on something they are passionate about. For some, including me, I needed someone to steer me in the right direction. That was when I figured I needed to work with someone and made the decision and the investment to work with Shawn Shewchuk. It might seem simple at first because many of us have the head knowledge of what we need to do, but sometimes it needs to be said that the head knowledge needs to be transferred to strategic intentions that are executed bit by bit and day by day to achieve the results that you want.

The mission of your business stems from your personal vision and your values. In many cases, the vision of the entrepreneur mirrors the vision of the business. Personally, when I was looking at my own life and my own purpose, three things came to mind.

- I am a child of God: I am wonderfully and purposefully made, and actions that I take align with my beliefs.
- I am a servant-leader: I am continuously serving my clients, my employees and associates to be the best that they can be.
- I am present: I make myself available as needed for my family, friends, clients and the people who work with me.

These were the first steps that I took towards narrowing down my passion, and they helped form the foundation of my business ventures. My work in consulting, coaching and training allows me to be present and serve a variety of businesses and individuals in many different settings, and I am grateful for the opportunity. Narrowing down these goal areas helped me identify some of the key objectives that I needed to see in my life and my business.

At the end of the day, what I loved about what I do is seeing my clients succeed in all of their ventures, whether it is starting out in their own business, charting a new course for their existing business, deciding how the business can generate more revenue, or scaling their business and preparing it for growth.

The choices and actions that I make daily hinge upon these three things that I hold dear to me and that excite me. I ask myself each time I make a decision or before I do or say things—*Does this align with the identity of the business and my three values that make me who I am?* If it does not, or if it stays in a 'gray' area, I will have to then decide what is the best course of action.

Everything that we do is based on the choices that we make every minute of every day. I have to make a choice and a decision to not hit the 'snooze' button in the morning. I must make a choice to put in at least a 30-minute workout every day. I must make a choice to spend at least ⅔ of my day building my business. I must make a choice to not yell at my son for spilling milk or dropping crumbs when he's eating. You must make a choice, and these choices are anchored on your values. Once you have a good foundation of your purpose, your vision, and your values, you are able to make decisions and choices based on that.

It takes time to build upon these values, and I continue to work on it. I don't believe for a second that there is a state that you get to where you have achieved your values, but these values become what you are; that becomes your business (pun intended), and your business is dependent on the clients that you are able to attract. If your clients can resonate with your values and you are able to solve their problems, your personal value will have gone up.

What problems can you solve?

All of us have a story to tell. We all lived through experiences of varying nature, and no one person is the same as the other. Every business starts with an idea such as improving a current product or service. The idea could be anything, and this is where many get stuck. Unfortunately, many entrepreneurs have great dreams and ideas, but they stagnate without a concrete vision of how to turn those dreams into reality.

Sometimes, a business idea may come accidentally. Cole was trying to hire a contractor to work on improving his garage but could not find a reputable contractor that does exactly what he wanted. He decided to buy the equipment and taught himself how to do it. Over time, he was bringing his equipment to work on his friends' and family's garages, and he started to build a reputation. He is now recognized as one of the top garage transformation companies in the area. In this case, he saw a problem, he went and learned how to solve it because no one could help him with it, and he created value for himself and for the people like him who needed the solutions only he could provide. His personal value increased. As he is able to solve bigger problems, his worth has increased even more.

Jim Collins, in his book *Built to Last: Successful Habits of Visionary Companies*, defines Big Hairy Audacious Goals (BHAG) as a "powerful mechanism for stimulating progress". It was said that Steve Jobs' BHAG was "To make a contribution to the world by making tools for the mind that advance humankind". Wow, that is certainly one BHAG. But guess what—he turned that goal into reality, and today humankind has certainly benefited from his goal. In Cole's case, all he wanted was to make over his garage, and he stumbled upon the opportunity to make other peoples' lives better.

Think of these vision statements from several brands that you might recognize:

TED: Spread ideas
Nike: Bring inspiration and innovation to every athlete
Prezi: To reinvent how people share knowledge, tell stories, and inspire their audiences to act
IKEA: To create a better everyday life for the many people
Google: To organize the world's information and make it universally accessible and useful

These are simple, profound, and compelling statements that state exactly what their organizations want to achieve. Vision statements do not need to be big blabbers. If you are not able to state (and remember) the vision of your company, then you need to take a serious look into what it is that you are able to contribute through your business.

My vision is to be the best dad to my two sons, the best husband to my wife, and to support my clients to live out their potential through meaningful work. My mission statement, which corresponds to the mission of my business, is simply "to make myself and others successful every day". Think of your business idea. What is the one problem that you can change to make the world a better place? How will you do that? That will be your mission statement. Take the time to answer this question.

Seeing the end

Mission and vision statements need to be aligned for any business. While your mission tells you what you are, a vision provides a clear and compelling direction of where you see yourself and your business at a certain time in the future.

How did you start your business? Was it a nudge or a whisper, or were you inspired to do something because of something you've seen? What did you do with the nudge or the whisper? Most importantly, did the whisper excite you and give you peace of mind?

I understand that when stunt car drivers are taught to do the 180 degree turns, they are asked to look over to where they want to see the car and visualize it being there instead of focusing on how to move the car 180 degrees. You have to see it for yourself and not doubt it. One of the measures that can be used to measure the success of a business is the revenue that you bring in. Perhaps your business is now making $25,000. What's stopping you from turning the $25k business into $100k? Why not $250k? Why even limit to $250k? Why not $1m? Remember, it all boils down to what you want, and, with that, how you will get there. Saying it's impossible right from the start is your permission to yourself to not get to that level of success.

So, what is the vision of your business and your life? As a business manager, is your mission to make money or to make a difference? There is nothing wrong with either mission, but you need to be committed and focused on it. If your intention is to make money, you will be evaluating opportunities that come your way with a financial lens. "What is the investment required?" and "When will I see the returns on my investment?" If your intention is to make a difference, the questions that you might ask then may be, "How will my business or my life be improved?"

At the end of the day, it is not about how much you bring home. I'll emphasize again that there's nothing wrong if your aim is to make more money. Personally, I live by the proverb that the love of money is the root of all evil. Money itself is an enabler for me to do what I desire to do. Not having to spend hours in front of the computer looking for cheap flights or being able to afford to contribute to make the world a better place, working with communities that need the support to help their people, or to make meaningful donations to the people who need the resources—those are my drivers. And I can't do any of that without the money that enables it to come true.

Perhaps another thought-starter would be the famous quote from Dan Sullivan, the author of *The Laws of Lifetime Growth*, where he asked, "If we were having this discussion three years from today, and you were to look back over those three years today, what has to have happened, both personally and professionally, for you to feel happy about your progress?"

Reflection

1. Develop your own vision and mission statement. Start by asking what your purpose is. Your role as a parent, employer, employee, contractor, etc.? How do you want to be seen by others?
2. What are the three things that you would do first, if you had the opportunity to earn $2m by tomorrow? How will that improve your life?
3. If I were to give you $2m to spend over the course of 48 hours, what would you spend it on?

Chapter 5 Leading in your business

We can't talk about business and entrepreneurship without talking about leadership. It is an essential quality that every business owner needs to have. Leadership does not mean bossing people around or that you need to have people reporting to you. It works in some cases, but not in the 21st century. Leadership is not positional power. It is about influence.

There has been countless literature written about leadership since the turn of the 20th century, and it is not the purpose of this book to add to the myriad of very good material written about this topic.

Many people get overwhelmed by the whole topic of leadership. Ultimately, it comes down to two things. Leadership is all about love, service and sacrifice. Power and authority have their place in leadership but love and service are what get you farther in influencing both yourself and others—and in getting things done when you want them done. For business leaders and entrepreneurs, these are essential skills that must be developed.

A common misconception is that some people are born leaders. If you are blessed enough to be born into a family of entrepreneurs and successful businesspeople, chances are that you are exposed to elements of risk-taking, leadership and running a business at an earlier age, so you may have an advantage over others at this.

Privilege also has its downfall if the proper upbringing is not put in place. You probably have heard about spoiled kids who spent their family fortune and did not end up with much. You have also heard of people who had nothing but rose from nothing to become successful leaders in whatever field they chose to be in.

I grew up in a middle-class family and always had what I needed and wanted. I had no lack growing up, and I also had the privilege of studying overseas. That said, although my parents had covered my tuition fees, I had to work to earn my keep, from flipping burgers, making sandwiches, driving international students to and from the airport and writing in the university newspaper. In all my years of growing up, I have always avoided being the leader. I did not mind being number two, but being a leader was something that I was not comfortable with. That is, until I parted ways with an employer and ventured into the world of entrepreneurship. I knew I had to take uncomfortable actions, and one of those uncomfortable actions was taking charge. Taking charge of me, my businesses, and my associates and employees.

I had to step up into becoming the leader that I did not think that I could be. I read self-help books, listened to audiobooks, took chances, and tried different methods. One of the best practices that helped me nurture my leader-within was being a member of LeaderImpact, a group where like-minded businesspeople get together to support and encourage each other in different areas of personal and leadership development. That is my mastermind group. On top of that, I work with a coach that would continually push me into uncomfortable zones and hold me accountable. Those were steps that I took to boost my self-confidence and leadership knowledge. Am I there yet? Heck no, I'm a work-in-progress, as we all are. But I can tell you, I'm not where I was, and I'm on my way to where I want to be.

What I have learned in this journey is how determined and disciplined I needed to be to achieve my goals. It doesn't matter how old you are or whether you had the privilege to be born into wealth. Everything can be learned.

This is the framework of leadership that helps me get to where I want to be, and I am still continually learning new methods, taking chances in implementing them, and improving and sharpening them constantly.

Leadership is about leading yourself

The first person that you need to learn to lead is yourself. Many people I know would agree with me that you are the hardest person that you'll ever experience in leading. I kept justifying to myself why I could not and would not accomplish something that I had set out to do. I kept looking at myself in the mirror and saying that I'm never going to be like that successful person—I am not good enough, I am not good looking enough, I am never going to have that skill to accomplish that, and so on. Remember, you are what you think you are.

In Shawn Shewchuk's book *Change Your Mind, Change Your Results*, he indicates that our minds are divided into two parts—conscious and subconscious. The conscious mind is what we are aware of and what we see and hear and experience every minute of the day. Decisions that we make every day are in the conscious part of our mind. It is where 'free will' comes to play; where we make choices to accept or reject thoughts. It's also where we choose to listen to a certain type of music, watch a certain type of film on television, or choose to listen to what others are saying about us. The ability to accept or reject is one of the most incredible virtues of a human being. Whatever we feed into our minds ultimately feeds into our subconscious minds and is stored for later use. It becomes the data centre for everything that is you; it is where your beliefs, past experiences, memories, and skills are—and everything that you have experienced.

Have you ever wondered why some music can cause an emotional response? Sometimes without your even knowing it? Random thoughts that vividly bring you back to an experience? Although it has been many years since I graduated from university, every so often when the radio station plays Meatloaf's "I'd Do Anything for Love" or "Two Out of Three Ain't Bad", it suddenly transports me to the time when I was at the university cafeteria, eating mushy mac-and-cheese and seeing Ken putting eight sachets of sugar into the already sweetened chocolate milk. That's because 97.7 The Wolf Classic Rock Station was always playing from the speakers, whether we liked it or not. It was always playing the same songs, day after day and sometimes several times a day. The repeated conditioning etched a spot in my subconscious, probably for the rest of my life!

Imagine you. What do you tell yourself every day? Do you affirm yourself every day? Dr. Wayne Dwyer had once said that when we change the way we look at things, the things we look at change. I can certainly relate to that. The first time I facilitated a workshop, I totally flopped. In the back of my mind, I was already telling myself that I was not going to do a good job, and guess what—I did not. My thoughts manifested themselves. Since that day, I made a conscious decision to tell myself that I am a great facilitator, and there are scores of people in the room waiting to be wowed by my presentations.

Leadership is about serving others

In this world that we live in, the 'leader' is usually the person that is holding a position of authority. One of the definitions of a 'leader' found in the Merriam-Webster dictionary is "a person who has commanding authority or influence". This definition of a leader is not incorrect because in society, even in the animal kingdom, there is always the one leader that makes the decision. There is only one conductor in an orchestra and only one President or Prime Minister of a country.

That said, the actions of a leader have somewhat evolved over the past 50 years. In leadership in the 21st century, a leader is the driver on a bus, and it is the leader's role to get his team on the bus and driving toward one destination. This is the visionary leader—one who knows where he or she needs to go and is able to get the team in on it. The other role of a leader is one of service. This is perhaps one of the traits of a leader that often gets overlooked, but, in my opinion, is one of the most crucial elements of who a leader should be. A leader should be someone who serves with humility by empowering, enabling, and supporting the team to execute.

Both of the traits of a leader are important. You cannot empower your team if you do not have a compelling vision to rally it, and you cannot use the stick approach with your team because all you will do is create a very unhappy team; the risk is that you might lose your people. The greatest example that I can think of as a successful servant leader is Jesus Christ. Before His crucifixion, He washed His disciple's feet, and one of His disciples, Peter, told Him, "You will never wash my feet." Jesus' response was, "If I do not wash your feet, you have no part with me". Not only that, He commanded them and inspired them to serve each other and all others. This group of individuals went on to change the course of history because they took to heart their leader's vision of bearing fruit and making disciples.

Think in contemporary terms about who you might associate as successful servant leaders that inspired their organization or a movement. Names such as Mother Teresa, Nelson Mandela, or Mahatma Gandhi may come to mind. These are people who were humble, believed in a cause, had dreams of a better world and worked hard every day to serve others, sacrificing themselves in order to get to their dreams of a more caring, just, and free society.

Some common characteristics of a servant leader might look like these:

- *Selfless:* One of the most important characteristics of a servant leader is that of selflessness. The servant leader almost always puts others first because when others succeed, the team succeeds. It is not about the leader and how he or she looks in front of others. It's always about the team.
- *Empathetic:* Servant leaders take the time and effort to learn to connect with others, and they genuinely feel and understand the feelings of others. They understand that their actions and words will impact more than themselves. Part of being empathetic is also being a good listener, especially in applying the skills of active listening and emotional intelligence to ensure that one takes the time to understand before being understood.
- *Aware:* Servant leaders may sometimes appear to look "weak" by our common societal standards, but they are always in tune and aware of everything that is going on around them. They may take actions strategically, aligning these actions with their values and achieving a bigger picture.

Leadership is about dreams and hopes

Throughout my career, I have never really thought about who I am or what I wanted to do. I studied Engineering in university because I thought that was cool, but I never really had a passion for it. My first career was in Information Technology; I could do the work and did it quite well but, again, it never became what I always wanted to do. Then, as my responsibilities grew, I started, not intentionally, getting into leading groups of people in different areas and, ultimately, ended up in Human Resources and Talent Management. Even then, it didn't seem like things clicked for me. When I bought my first business and started to facilitate training programs that helped people be more productive – to do more with less and to use desktop tools more effectively – I became more passionate in what I do, although I was still lacking something that I could not identify. I knew that I loved helping people, and I loved seeing them do well because of what I had shown them, and when I was given the opportunity to support various communities to overcome adversity and societal problems, that's when I had the epiphany – that I was able to make a difference and to contribute to better a society

Since that moment, I've been continually looking at opportunities to reach out to more people that I can help and turning that into my new-found career. Too often, when people are thinking of hopes and dreams, they think of wealth, status, power, and comfort. The only problem is, how much wealth is enough for you to get to where you want to be? There is always the next shiny new thing. What if we dreamt of having closer relationships? What if we dreamt of being more spiritual, building a community, supporting each other, finding peace and having a better quality of life? I get that in many cases you need material gains to support everything that you dream about, but the focus is about what the material wealth is able to do for you, not how much money you will make.

Leadership is being proactive

Dreams and hopes will remain if they are not turned into action. After determining where the end goal is for your dream, you will need to prepare with intensity and develop a detailed plan on where and how you will get there. It is all in the execution. You can plan all you want, but if there is poor execution, you will not arrive at your goals.

Being proactive means you need to plan. You may be familiar with the Important vs. Urgent matrix, made famous by Stephen Covey. Very often, we find ourselves working on Urgent matters that are not necessarily Important because we fail to take the time to plan. We run from one shiny new object to the next shiny new object. In the case of the entrepreneur, from one opportunity to the next. This is reacting to the situation. We are not taking charge and not following a plan. I know this because I have been there. After a while, you start losing focus on what you are really meant to be doing, because of all the 'noise' and 'voices' telling you that there's a better opportunity knocking, and you have to take action now or it will be gone forever. We fail to take the time to align the new opportunities with our own values and vision.

Being proactive means you are always at the forefront of the industry that you are in. Read literature regarding your business and learn about new tools that will benefit you. I have clients who refused to advance themselves, giving themselves excuses not to learn technology because "I am old school". That's not an excuse. It is about staying relevant. If you have problems learning a technology, speak to your kids or your grandkids, or enrol in a course to get you the help you need.

Leadership is about influence

Everyone influences someone in one way or another every day. It does not matter what position of authority you are in—whether you are the CEO or the janitor. At some point in time, we are all influencers. Sometimes a young CEO may go to the seasoned janitor for advice, and there's absolutely no wrong in that because the janitor who has been in the company for years may have some gray matter about the culture of the organization—much more than the new head of the company.

As leaders, we do not have the right to force our opinion on others, and this goes both ways. Our focus should be on: how do we bring the team together, what does our communication with each other need to look like, what does service to client mean?

Leadership today is very much a collaborative approach rather than a top-down driven approach, and there should not be any force or authority when it comes to leading with influence. The first purpose of leading through influence is the willingness to engage with all the people who will be impacted by what we do.

Priority Management's 3-D model of work explains this perfectly.

1. Decide: This is where we decide what needs to be done—how it aligns with the ultimate goal and the plan that will take us there. This is the strategic aspect of any work.
2. Do: This is where we get things done through management of priorities and resources and the assignment of tasks to ensure that they are done accordingly to plan.
3. Deliver: When the work is done, it needs to be delivered, and this is where the ability to influence becomes vital. This is where the true value of the work needs to be communicated and realized to the right stakeholders, who

will receive the work. If you executed the best work but did not use the right influencing skills, your work may not be given its true value.

When we think of influence, we sometimes refer to it as an on-off button. We can influence someone when we need to—the reality is we cannot influence anyone on a whim. Influencing is a skill that needs to be nurtured and developed over time. Think about your own children. Can you switch on your 'Influence' switch and say, "I now want to influence you to clean the dishes"? It doesn't work that way. This is a learned skill that needs to continue to be nurtured and built over time.

Leadership is about confidence and having a winning attitude

As we saw in the previous two chapters, having a good character, a strong vision and an executable plan is important for a leader to succeed. With these characteristics, coupled with a clear executable vision, you will begin to build confidence. Why do some sport teams continue to have a winning streak, while some continue to dwell in the basement of rankings for some time before something changes, either with the coaching personnel or team members? It's all about creating a winning attitude and an executable plan to achieve the singular goal—winning games and championships. It's the same in business—there are no quick fixes. Winning and being successful is hard work and there is no easy solution to it. You can ease parts of your business, which we will talk about in later chapters, but determination, grit and decisiveness are the key ingredients to building confidence. Once you have achieved a win, you will continue to build on that streak, to continue winning and repeating the work.

Collaboration in leadership and in business

As a business owner, you are always leading; either leading yourself or leading your team. If you are not leading, you are part of a tribe or you are working for somebody who is giving you instructions on what to do next. As a leader, you need to have the intuitiveness of when to collaborate, when to work together with others, and when to lead.

Collaboration is not about following unless it is referred to as 'following a tribe'. You may have someone on social media that you 'follow', or an entity with which you identify because it aligns with your belief systems. You may be part of a Bob Proctor tribe, a Christ tribe, a Climate Change tribe. You may work yourself in to be part of that tribe or that group, and your actions are aligned with what the tribe says you should do.

When I work on a project with a group of people to put something together, we are all coming together collaboratively. There are rules to follow, of course; everyone plays a different role in the group. You need to have a leader, a coordinator, specialists, administrators, and so on. In this world and age, you are never working alone, unless you are a narcissist and self-centred individual. Everything that we do today is part of something bigger. Self-centredness is not a leadership quality. It is an individual quality that proclaims, "I do not need anyone else to succeed". That just plain does not work.

As a leader, you need to be able to flex your style, depending on who your audience is. It is about when and how to lead, not when to follow. Click!Colours is a tool that I have used extensively with many clients to help them discover their personality and leadership qualities—for themselves and for their teams. It also helps leaders to flex their leadership styles, depending on who they are working with, to ensure that proper styles and leadership techniques are used in the right circumstances.

Reflection

1. Think of a leader with whom you had the opportunity to work in the past and who had impacted you positively. What did he/she do that made that impact?

2. Reflecting on the qualities that we have described in this chapter, which are the areas that you need to work on? Name three tasks that you will do first to help you address your areas of improvement.

Chapter 6 Overcome self-doubt and just do it

The last chapter in this section of developing the business plan is on execution. You may have the best vision, values and mission statement, and you may also be a great influencer and have a sharp focus on where you want to be in 24 months. All that will come to naught if you do not execute.

Execution is key to getting the outcome you desire. You may have heard that you should take more time to plan than to execute, but if you do not execute the plan that you created, you will not achieve the results that you deserve, want and desire.

Priority Management teaches a simple rule called the Productivity Formula. It simply says:

Tasks + Processes + Tools = Results

To get the results that you want, you need to have all three elements. You need to focus on the task at hand, using the right kind of process and having the right tools. If you lack any of these, you will not get the right kind of results. Bear in mind, the tools that we are referring to here are not necessarily physical tools like a hammer, but could be soft tools as well, such as a spreadsheet or a framework.

More importantly, you need to understand that having all the right tools and processes is not going to get you there if you're not focused on doing the right things. There are many reasons why we are not always executing right; here are some of them.

You are always connected

The digital world that we live in today has advanced humankind by leaps and bounds. Information is at our fingertips. We can binge-watch an entire series of TV shows in one sitting instead of waiting anxiously, for 'must-see-Thursdays', and we can watch it from anywhere and on many devices. But guess what—our devices and their constant availability to connect us to the world is a huge distraction in executing our plans. Do you, like I used to, wake up in the morning with your device on hand—checking the latest posting and, throughout the day, checking on the news, viral videos and social media rants, or just watching silly animal videos? Have you ever used the phone apps that track the time that you are on your device? It is a scary thought if you put it in perspective.

We spend at least one-third of our days on our devices, with the justification that we need to keep ourselves up to date. These things suck our attention away from more important things. They suck our attention and reduce our ability to focus and do high-leverage activities. They are our excuse for not doing other things. As I am writing this, I am also writing to myself and reminding myself of the detrimental effects of staying connected. Although the digital world can feel liberating at times, such as having instant answers to pretty much anything that you want to know in the world, our attention span takes a back seat because of information overload and the abundance of choices that present itself to us every minute of every day.
It's also not always about the live streams and social media feeds. Many people, me included, are also fighting a deluge of emails,

phone calls and texts throughout the day. Many of the people that I work with have to deal with hundreds of emails a day, and that's average. Let's break that down. If you are receiving 100 emails a day, that's an average of 12.5 emails every hour, based on an 8-hour workday. That's almost 5 minutes per email. I get it—some emails are worth only a 2-second look, but still, it takes away valuable time. In this new knowledge economy, we are distracted every 11 minutes, and it takes over 20 minutes to really get our heads back to where we were. No wonder we don't get things done or don't do them effectively.

Have you ever felt the elation when you received mail from a long-lost friend? How about when AOL first came out with "You've got mail"? Everyone got excited because someone sent them an email. Dopamine, the 'pleasure' chemical, springs into action. Each time a 'ping' arrives, we are conditioned to need to check the email, until this becomes what we are. Years of conditioning take discipline to get undone. I have clients that I have worked with who have said, "My work is my emails, and, based on our SLA (Service Level Agreement) with our clients, these have to be responded to and acted on within the hour". I get that we need to meet SLAs, but how do you strike a balance between resolving an incident that you received 10 minutes ago and needing to take action on another incident that just came in seconds ago? Where would you put your focus? But, unfortunately, that's the way that people have been conditioned.

Fear that it won't go well

You may have the most beautiful and perfect plan that you looked over and over yesterday. When it's time to wake up in the morning to execute it, you start to experience cold feet. Maybe I shouldn't call Suzie because she might say, "No". Or, "I don't know if I can actually do this". Perhaps you start to doubt that your idea may not be the best, or you think someone has already done something similar and has been doing it for years before you came on the scene.

These are examples that I can relate to because I have experienced them, and I continue to better myself by swimming upstream to overcome these challenges. The problem with being a perfectionist is that we don't get things done until we are very sure that it's going to succeed. We all know the trouble with that; we all have the head knowledge of what it is.

We may also be over-analyzing a situation. How many times do you have to analyze before it turns into analysis-paralysis? We overthink a situation until it paralyzes us and stops us from moving forward. Here's an example. If you keep thinking about Suzie saying "No" to your request for her business, chances are she will likely say "No". What happens next? Many entrepreneurs will continue to analyze what went wrong and why Suzie said "No", instead of moving on to the next prospect. Remember, not everyone is a client. You need to be able to discriminate and understand the reality that you won't do business with everyone that you meet. There are those out there who would love to do business with you. But unless you are out there reaching out to more people, you will remain an unknown.

Not knowing where to start

Many times, when we are writing up business strategies, we are not detailed enough to see the actual tasks and activities that are required to achieve the results. When the detailed tasks are not clearly written, that's when things can start to go awry. You won't know where to start, or when to start, and where the end goals are. Many entrepreneurs that I know do not like documentation. We fail to document what we did, how we did it, to whom we reached out and when we need to reach out to that prospect again. We may have all the tools in the world, but when we do not use them to their fullest, it's still garbage.

If you are not driven by data, you can't measure your progress. How many calls did you make today? How many appointments did you make? How many of those appointments turned into clients for you? If you are making five calls a day, chances are you won't reach the number that you need to have the volume of clients that you'd like to have.

James is an owner of a restaurant. His goal is that he wants to make $1M in revenue to continue to be in the game, pay off his loans, and still be able to take home some money for himself and afford to travel to Europe for a week with his family. His business depends solely on dine-in customers, take-out and some delivery. He needs to sell about $2,800 per day (based on the restaurant being opened 355 days a year) to make that happen. His marketing plans include posting weekly specials on social media and displaying images of the delicious meals that he sells. He also has a few ads on the radio and the local paper.

He starts to plan his week. Every week, he plans what he intends to do every day. As things get busy, he tends to neglect some of the daily tasks that have to take place to keep the business operational. Over time, he begins to work more and more in the business, and he stops dreaming about what the business could be because he stopped planning and measuring.

This is very common among business owners. You default to continue to work in the business instead of working to *build* the business. Dilemmas such as, "We do not have enough people" or "We can't afford another employee" come to mind. Not knowing how to scale a business to meet future needs and not keeping up to date on consumer trends are the most familiar problems for an entrepreneur and business owner.

Overcome self-doubt

This is where many entrepreneurs stumble. This is where I had stumbled many times. I had the greatest plans for how each of my businesses would go, and I had aimed at the goal too many times. What I needed to do was to pull the trigger. I struggled so many times in my entrepreneurial career that when it came time to take action, I sometimes chickened out.

"I'm not good enough"
"Someone stole my idea"
"I don't feel like doing this today"
"If it's that great of an idea, somebody somewhere must have already done something with it"

Those were some of my feelings when I did not execute my plans. I justified why. When that happens, guess what—your plans are useless. Failing to deliver is perhaps the biggest impediment to success. One of my reasons for not taking action is that the task is overwhelming, and feelings like "I don't think I can do this" spring to mind. It's way out of my comfort zone.

What I have learned is that no matter how uncomfortable a certain action could be, it is still worth doing. I do not have to wait for perfection to do something. If I am waiting for that perfect alignment of the moon, star and Mars, I'll be waiting a long time.
I have learned, through hardships and earning road rashes along the way, that it doesn't have to be this way. It is hard, that's for sure, but 90% of success is hard work—doing it every day, with a passion, and learning to pivot when you need to.

Have you ever participated in a workshop, summit or conference of any kind and gotten super excited about the prospect of changing your life, business and everything else in between, only to realize that after the 3-day summit, where you learned to walk on fire and overcome all sorts of objections, you have to go back to your regular life? Did the doubt that you thought you had overcome suddenly hit you like a tonne of bricks? That's one of the limiting beliefs that you will need to overcome to be successful in whatever you do. There is a simple but very effective framework that I have used; I have also used it with clients to overcome some of this self-doubt. It all starts with having a plan and making an irrevocable decision. It is a non-terminable contract that you sign with yourself and consider a life-and-death situation.

Here is a framework that you can use to properly take your plan to the finish line:

Plan → Gain capability to execute → Take action to execute

Plan

Whenever you are applying for a business loan or a grant, one of the first things that you are asked is whether you have a business plan. The bank or the funding institution wants to know that you know what you're doing. TV shows like "Shark Tank" and "Dragons' Den" are filled with investors wanting to give away money to good ideas that bring good returns. They don't just give money away for a good idea. They want to know what you have done or are planning to do to grow that business. What do you think will happen if pilots do not have a flight plan plotted out? Or a destination to go to?

I have known many people who get into business because they have an interest in a certain area. That works in some cases, but it gets you only so far. Instead of reporting to another person in the office, you just created a job for yourself—reporting to yourself. How many times have you heard of that friend or a friend of a friend who is a really good cook who opened a restaurant, only to work in the business day and night, stressed, and end up closing the business because it was too much to handle, and there were so many aspects of a business that they did not take into account?

I would like to stress two things here. You need a plan for yourself—what you want to achieve in life. Do you have a concise goal that you want to achieve for yourself? What does that look like? What are some key areas that you would like to achieve? Think of your own personal goals in these functional areas: Spiritual, Physical, Relationships, Job/Career, etc. For example, if you have "Develop a strong relationship with spouse" as a relationship goal, what are some key activities that you need to do in order to achieve that? It could be spending time everyday to speak with them, going on date nights regularly, be grateful everyday for them and making sure that they know it, and making it a priority at all times.

As for your business, it needs to have a goal too. What does that goal look like? It must go beyond monetary value. What is it that you would like to achieve with the success of your business? For this exercise, you need to close your eyes for a moment.

Picture yourself forward by 24 months from the time you are reading this. At the end of the 24 months, your business is a success, and you have met every goal and perhaps even exceeded some. Think back to 24 months before and answer the following questions:

- What has that success done for you?
- What challenges have you overcome for you to have achieved that success?
- What are others saying about your successes?

- What processes of your life could be emulated and repeated for continued success, or to share with others?

That is where you need to start. Having a clear, concise picture of what that success looks like. Then reverse engineer that to what needs to happen for your business. In addition to your vision, mission and values, you need to start considering how you are planning to run your business, and who will be involved in the day-to-day operations? Where can I get funding? What kind of financing should I plan for? What is the cash flow needed to ensure the business is sustainable? What is the cost of my products or services? How much should I charge? Where are my customers coming from? Where do they hang out (online and physically)? What do they need? How do they think? What is the ideal age range of my customers? What are they suffering from? How can I help them to overcome their challenges? How much should I need monthly and weekly to ensure that I have sufficient money to keep the business open?

Build capability

You may have all the needed capability for planning your business, but this is where many people fall down. It's about following through with your plan with a level of dogged focus. You need to start gaining the capability to work your plan. It might mean learning a new technology, even when you are 65; it might mean registering yourself for self-improvement training or it might mean going back to school. It means different things to different people. This is all about you finding where your own gaps are and finding ways to fill those gaps—maybe by using available resources such as a business or life coach to help you steer yourself the right way, get to the right thinking and have a blueprint for success, while encouraging and handholding you along the way. It might also be signing up to get trained on a topic to get you up to speed or certified so you are able to do the work effectively. Another way to gain capability is to hire the right people to work on a job that you need done. Remember, you do not have to go it alone. A lot of entrepreneurs who work for themselves (I usually refer to them as the solopreneurs) sometimes find it discouraging. They are all they've got, and they do not have the necessary support system. This is where working with a coach or belonging to a group of like-minded people will help steer them in the right direction to keep on building their own capability. Stop getting thick in the head; humble yourself and seek the help that you need. There is no shame in reaching out to get better at what you do. That in itself is strength.

Gaining capability also extends to your immediate support system—your family and your personal life. If all you focus on is your business, your family life is going to take a hit. On the other hand, if your family and personal life are in a mess today, your business is also going to suffer. Are there areas in your life that need to be worked on? Are you happy in your marriage? Gain the capability and get the resources to fix those problems if they need to be fixed. This is essential to your success.

Take action

When you were in school, and your exams were in three days, if you were like me you would spend the last couple of nights reviewing materials so that you could regurgitate them for the exam. I would not advise you to follow in these footsteps but, in a way, that was accountability. I knew what I had to do and by when, although not the best way to get there. But you get my point. When you are in a job, you are given a task to complete or your pay will be affected. Or if your child has to go for hockey practice at 4 pm every Wednesday, you will find a way, or an alternative for Wednesdays, so you can get them to practice on time. We tend to be accountable when things are on the line and we are given no choice. If you are an employer today, one thing that you cannot possibly postpone is payroll. It does not matter if you pay your employees twice a month or once a month—when it's payroll time, you will make sure that it gets done to avoid getting embarrassing phone calls when your people are not paid on time.

Somehow, when it comes time for entrepreneurs to build their businesses, many tend not to work on the important, but less urgent, matters—activities that are strategic in nature and activities that would grow and scale the business. Many business owners are caught in the daily operations, administration and running of the business instead of the growing cycle of the business. This could also be due to the fact that many business owners are not sure how to get to the next level. You might know in your mind where you want to see your business, but you may not have the gumption to get it going.

I know I have my fair share of problems with accountability. I would make a list of people I want to reach out to, but when it comes time to call, I find myself more than one excuse why I should not be talking to this person or that one.

What I have learned over my years of being in business is that I do not have to wait for the perfect timing to do certain things—because there is no perfect time. When my clients ask, "When is a good time to start a business? Should I start my business now during the pandemic? What type of business do I want to be in?", my answer is, "There is no better time than now to start your business or pivot your business". I'll qualify my answer. If you think that you need to take your business in a different direction, or if you want to start a side business, the best time to do it is now. 'Now' means you will also begin to look at where you would like your business to be, what value you will be adding to your clients, what products you want to sell, what revenue you want to generate, and some of the other components that we talked about in the previous chapters. Right after doing the required analysis, and if you're comfortable with where you're at (remember it doesn't have to be perfect, because no plan is perfect), you need to make a promise to yourself, and this promise is an Irrevocable Decision, meaning that you cannot run away from it. It is as if someone has a gun pointed at your head, and you do not have a choice but to move with your plan. If given a choice, most people would choose to go the easy way out—the easy way to make money. But unless you were born into wealth or win a lottery ticket, there is no easy way. It takes effort to be successful, and it begins with accountability in execution.

Nothing happens to your business, and you will not see the results of your dream if the execution is not carried out properly, timely, and with as much precision and focus as possible.

Take small, calculated steps

If you aim at nothing, you will hit it every time. When Apollo 11 was on its way to the moon in 1969, it was not flying a direct path from Earth to Moon. There were thousands of course corrections before it made its way to its destination. A tiny error in calculation could have been detrimental to the mission. But Apollo 11 ultimately reached the moon. The mission was a success because the goal was reached.
It is the same with business. Aim for the destination but be flexible to make course corrections as needed to get you to where you want to be. When you plan, you need to ensure that the plan itself is not overwhelming or it will stop you right from the start.
If James were to look at his end goal – that he needs to generate $1m in 12 months – most people would look at that number and doubt themselves, mainly because they have not seen that kind of

money. But if he were to break it down to $2,800 a day, it may not seem that unreachable. If he opens his business for 8 hours a day, that's $350 per hour that he needs to bring in to make his goal. That would mean he needs to have an average of 20 customers per hour, each spending $17.50. Of course, some hours he will have more than 20, and some hours of the day he will have fewer. His marketing efforts will now be focused on generating 20 customers every hour. These customers are generated via different channels—traditional media, social media, word of mouth, referrals and mail-in specials. A complete analysis could then determine which channel would bring him the 'biggest bang for the buck'. Customer segmentation will come into play when this happens, and a few other analytics.

The bottom line is, think big but work your way down to small, bite-sized executables that will allow you to see smaller, shorter-term goals. Don't be so overwhelmed by the big hairy audacious goals that you lose sight of the smaller gains that you need to make to achieve the end destination.

Where would you start?

Take a step back. No matter where you are in your life now, you have the experience, the knowledge and the scars to show for you to be where you are today. Think of these life experiences as something that you can showcase. Showcase it through your business—to your employees and to your clients. Someone out there needs what you have.

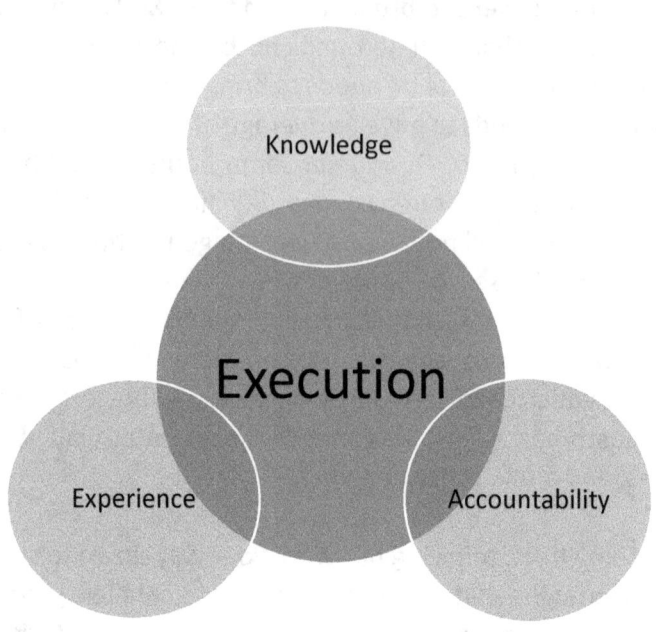

As the diagram shows, it all comes down to execution. You need the experience and the knowledge, and measures of success that you will hold yourself accountable, but ultimately, it comes down to having to execute on your plans.

In the last few chapters, we have spent considerable time reflecting on the past and looking to the future. Now it's time that we start putting those visions and plans into gear. This is, by far, going to be your most difficult step. It's not hard to think of some lofty goals and plan on how to get there, but when it comes time to actually pick up the phone or sign on the dotted line for a loan, that's where many people get cold feet.

Start with the big picture

The tasks that you do every day – the seemingly menial tasks like picking up the phone, putting up a Facebook post, browsing the news, organizing a staff meeting, or even sleeping in – are choices that we make every day. Ask yourself these questions as you plan your day:

1. Are the tasks that I'm planning to do (or am doing now) linked to the bigger picture of my goals?
2. If they are not, why am I doing this (or that) task?
3. What is the implication for me in not focusing on the tasks that I know I need to do?
4. When will I achieve the results that I want if I do (or don't do) the tasks that I know I need to do?
5. What time of the day should I be focusing on high-leverage activities (tasks that give me the biggest bang for the buck)?

As a restaurant owner, James lives a very stressful and time-consuming life. But he has managed to develop a system and a plan for himself that is bite-sized, and he links to his big picture to see success in his business. A typical day for him looks like this:

6:00am - 7:00am: Devotion/meditation to get himself ready for the day
7:00am - 8:00am: Workout or gym
8:00am - 8:45am: Eat breakfast
8:45am - 9:00am: Travel to work
9:00am - 10:00am: Check on inventory, supplies and cleanliness of the kitchen, storage and dining areas
10:00am - 10:30am: Finalize a daily plan with the staff. Confirm the specials of the day, assign tasks, finalize shifts (in case of last-minute changes), prepare catering orders and tend to other last-minute preparations
10:30am - 11:00am: Final checks, food preparation
11:00am - 3:00pm: Serve lunch crowd dine-in and take-out

3:00pm - 4:30pm: Clean the dining area and prepare for dinner
4:30pm - 5:00pm: Check and respond to any emails and voicemails that may have come in during the day
5:00 - 6:00pm: Update social media posts (plan/time posts for the next day or next few days)
5:00pm - 10:00pm: Serve dinner crowd dine-in and take-out
9:00pm - 10:00pm: Check inventory and place any orders required for the next day (or next few days)
10:00pm: Kitchen closes, final check for the day
10:00pm - 10:30pm: Cash-up from the day

That's his typical day. James is only about a year into his business, so it does require a lot more of him, and his hours can be long. As his business stabilizes, he will have the resources to hire more people to do more of the administrative tasks. Then he can 'let go' of the business to focus on his family and continue growing his business.

As James can testify, running a business is hard work and takes a lot of effort, especially at the beginning stages. But I would say that almost everyone that I've worked with, who had at some point in their lives said that it was definitely a very rewarding experience, has never regretted that decision.

It is something that should not be taken lightly, but once you are in, you should put both feet in and be fully immersed in it. If you start to doubt, or to think you probably need the safety net of a job before you get started, you are not all in.

Reflection

1. What are the top three excuses that you give yourself for not achieving or doing what will make you successful?

2. What is stopping you from overcoming these self-doubts that you have?

3. Take a moment to think—if you were to eliminate one of the self-doubts that you have listed, how would it change the way you approach things? What if you took off the table another doubt that is stopping you?

4. Based on the self-doubts that you have listed, what are some small, calculated steps that you could take today to challenge yourself? What is that one irrevocable decision that you will make today?

Chapter 7 Building results-based habits

For many years, I had been groomed to think that hard work is the most important ingredient in making your career a success. I consider myself a great student while in grade school, and I'd like to think that I had a pretty successful few years in university, achieving a master's degree in electrical engineering and, later on, an MBA. Hard work and persistence for me meant studying into the wee hours of the morning, memorizing as much as possible, and regurgitating that information during exams. When I was 14, I was preparing for my Grade 8 piano exams. I remembered practising upwards of 8-10 hours a day, perfecting the three pieces of music and scales that I needed to do well in my 15-minute exam.

I continued to work hard at the jobs I had, but I never really saw the same kind of success that I had seen when I was in school, in a structured environment where I was told exactly what I needed to do in order to succeed. Well, in the real world, that is not the case. Working hard, focusing on what I was good at, practising and practising even harder works to an extent, but it does not take you all the way to the finish line that you desire for yourself. I started reading motivational books to find out what else I had to do. I was told that an attitude of gratitude and a "stick-to-it" attitude is also key to success. Well, I tried that, and it only got me a little further ahead. When I decided to work for myself and build up my own business, things got a little messier. I did not quite have the full grasp of what it really takes to build a business from scratch. There was no one above me telling me what my deliverables were, and I was pretty much left on my own to figure things out. Fortunately for me, I had the opportunity to work with a mentor and coach who helped me work some things out as I embarked on this new adventure of being an entrepreneur.

Through trial-and-error, I have found a few tips that have been effective for me personally and my business:

1. Be laser-focused about your future

This is possibly the most important part of building results-based habits. If you do not know where you are going, whether in life or in business, how will you know when you have arrived? Many of my clients have this as their single biggest problem. "I want to start my own business, but I'm not sure what success looks like for me." Use SMART goals (Specific, Measurable, Attainable, Relevant, Time-Based). Be very clear about your goals. If it's $250,000 that you would like to earn in the next 12 months, be specific about how you will measure that, what products or services you would like to sell, how relevant they are in the marketplace, and if your goal is realistic.

The next thing you need to do is to be very intentional and turn those intentions into specific actions. Remember the adage, "What gets scheduled gets done"? This is key. If you are serious about your goals, review them at the start and end of every day and journal your actions. How specific can you get? Are you satisfied with your daily performance? Do you have a clear idea of how your daily goals are linked to your goal in 12 months? If they are not, then you have to start making the decision to eliminate (or at least reduce) the distractions that are coming your way daily.
Some businesses (particularly network marketing businesses) would show pictures of a tropical vacation or a sexy new car that

you can drive, because someone already made it there and you can too!

There's nothing wrong with that kind of visioning. It does motivate some people to really get off their behind and do the work, but you have to be the one to ask yourself, "How is that important for me?"

Some questions that you can ask yourself concerning being laser-focused are:

a. How much do I want my business to bring in at the 12-month mark? At the 24-month mark? Or how much weight can I lose in 12 months? This is not to be a 'kinda' moment like, "I kinda want to make X amount of money in 12 months". Be specific.
b. What am I not clear of regarding my goals? Is it not important enough for me?
c. What do I have to do to clarify the gray areas of my goals?
d. Where am I lacking (whether it is in skills or attitude)? What can I do to fix it?
e. What does my future self tell my current self about what made me successful? In one minute, what can my future self tell my current self about what made me overcome the challenges that I faced?
f. If my heart were to stop beating in 12 months, what would people say about me?

2. Plan your priorities

Based on the first habit of being laser-focused, you now need to take that one step further and start looking at your priorities. What is important for you? Managing priorities is all about planning. Planning goes into every aspect of our lives. When we don't plan, our day will still go on, but it's just too unintentional; someone else planned it for us. That someone could be social media or you reacting to something or getting stressed because you haven't achieved what you said you want to achieve—when you didn't really set out to achieve anything other than that figment of imagination in your head. This is when things get busy for you, but you have nothing to show for it.

Some questions to consider as you are:

a. Do you normally plan your meetings? What outcome would you like to achieve at each of your meetings with whomever you are meeting with? Or is it meeting just to meet?
b. Do you plan your date nights with your significant other? Why not? If it is that important to you, it needs to be on your schedule.
c. Have you planned your talking points for your next client meeting, a meeting with a supplier or a prospect that you are working on?
d. Do you have a personal improvement plan (skills you want to develop) for what you're working on? Is it on your schedule?

It is important that we plan everything. When I teach WorkingSm@rt in Meetings, I use a Meeting Planner® to ensure that things do not get missed. I tell meeting chairs that they need to take the time to plan a meeting, so they do not just go into a meeting without any clear agenda or outcome. The typical feedback I get is that this is too cumbersome, and it takes too much time. Well, if you think it takes too much time to plan the meeting, think about the results that you will get if you *don't* plan—and the time spent discussing it during the meeting!

I get it. Sometimes the plan does not always go according to the plan. This is where you need to be flexible in preparing your fixed and flexible list. Fixed schedules should be on your calendar, whether it is your Outlook Calendar, Google Calendar, or just your faithful old little black book. Your tasks and to-do lists are your flexible schedule, which you can work on any time of the day.

If you are meeting a potential business client, you need to do your homework as well. Having a script is great, but you need to personalize it so that it means something to the person you are planning to speak with. Anticipate the interaction and put yourself in your prospect's shoes. It's like a game of chess—you need to think about your 'opponent' and your responses to it. When you are in that meeting, it is all about meeting the client's needs. We will talk more about the sales process in later chapters.

In planning, always leave about a 20 – 30% 'white space' that allows you to schedule your unscheduled tasks. If the white space does not end up getting used, then you can start looking at the next day's list and begin working on that. Most importantly, do not beat yourself up when things don't go according to how you planned it. Just look at what went wrong and start anew the next day. The sun always shines.

3. Be clear about your feelings

Not many people realize it, but sometimes what we think we want is what we think other people would *want* us to want. That's been my life for many years. Being successful meant having a good job and a good boss so that there is stability in life. There is no such thing as a loyal company. I had a good job, but was the extent, a job. I wasn't finding fulfilment in it because it didn't mean anything to me. It wasn't because I couldn't do the job – I did it quite well – but still, I wasn't happy. I tried going into another field and still didn't find the fulfilment that I was longing for. I was hopping from one job to the next, from one place to the next, trying to find that elusive 'great job'.

That was when I started to explore my feelings. What made me feel accomplished? I realized that seeing other people succeed was what motivated me. When my clients come up to me and say that I changed their lives – they do not live in their Inbox anymore, they are now less stressed because of the processes that I shared with them, and their projects are now more successful because they took the time to plan before execution – that makes my work fulfilling. When I am able to bring my clients to a place where they can find their own fulfillment, that makes what I do worthwhile. That changed my mindset from "I have to" to one that says, "I get to". I get to make a difference in another person's life. That is the motivation that I needed to stay ahead of the game and to stay ahead of myself before I brought myself down. Think about what you do that motivates you and takes you to a place where you find joy. If you have been a follower of Marie Kondo, you might relate to what 'sparks joy' in your life. Sparking joy is what will bring meaning to you and grow the feelings that you desire and deserve in your life. This joy is what also energizes you. As you think about what brings you energy, you need to also identify what pulls that joy away from you and think to yourself, *What do I need to do to lose that tension or take that 'negative energy' away from me?*

4.   Take care and plan time for yourself

Often, when we are in business, work gets prioritized. If you own a small business with only a few employees, and one of them calls in sick, it is most likely that you as the business owner will have to step in for the period. That's just one example of the ad-hoc stuff that 'attacks' the business owner constantly. When these unplanned activities occur, many times you take a back seat. When things get out of hand, sometimes you may feel like you have no time to have a meal or time to go for a walk. Taking care of yourself means a few things—that you are prioritizing your physical, mental and spiritual state.

    a. Be physically fit: Set time aside to be fit. Sixty minutes a day for 5 -6 days. If you think about that, you are investing 4% of a 24-hour day to keeping yourself healthy physically. Join a gym or subscribe to the countless online/streaming fitness programs that will keep you at optimal health. Where possible, you may even consult your family doctor to get a full-body checkup and work with them to optimize a workout program. You may even work with a nutritionist or a fitness trainer to get you to the fitness goals that you want. One of the most effective ways to get you off your chair or couch is to work with either a personal trainer or a workout buddy who will be there for you to 'kick you' and hold you accountable. Exercise is one of those things that mean the more you push yourself, the more energy you gain in the long run.

    b. Eat healthily: I have known many entrepreneurs who thrive and survive on snacks, eating at their desks and generally not having the proper nutrition. Like exercise, this is one of the areas that take time to think about and prepare for. It's so much easier to reach for the bag of chips that's readily available. Some that I know even don't drink enough water just because going to the bathroom means losing precious moments of work! Again, it's all about your priority. Fitness and nutrition go hand-in-hand. My wife works as a personal trainer and health coach. Part of her training program includes identifying what her clients are feeding themselves by having them log the foods and snacks that they consume every day. Many of her clients get the shock of their lives when they actually write down what they eat and when they eat it. Yes, it does take time to prepare a healthy meal and to pack a healthy sandwich for lunch. And yes, going to the bathroom will take a few additional minutes. But the benefits of keeping a healthy and fit life is second to none. My personal experience is that when I'm following and adhering to an exercise and fitness regime, my brain automatically does not want to even think about eating unhealthy food because that doesn't give me the nutrition and energy that I need to work out.

c. Volunteer in the community: There is something about serving that gives us satisfaction. For too long, especially in Western society, our brains have been wired for the "What's-in-it-for-Me?" syndrome. For some, the reason that they give is so that they can expect something back. Some give to the church hoping that their returns will be a hundred-fold. That is absolutely the wrong kind of thinking. Whenever I have the opportunity to participate in, or give to, an organization, knowing that my energy and resources go to help the less fortunate does give me a sense of being a contributor to the community that I live in or have an impact on. Volunteer and serve at a local church, the food bank, a service-oriented organization such as Rotary International or other similar organizations. In addition to meeting great people, it is an opportunity to take your mind off your business and to lend your skills for making a difference in your community.

5. Create a sense of urgency

Imagine this scenario. One of your loved ones is kidnapped, and the kidnapper points a gun to their head and tells you that you need to come up with a large sum of money in 24 hours, or that will be the last time that you will see your loved one. Reporting to the authorities aside, what do you think you will do? I know without a doubt that I will be out there using all sorts of methods available to me to get the money because a life depends on it.

This probably isn't the best example because it necessitates a reaction and a negative feeling. The reason I used this example is that when we are pushed to a corner, we have three choices—fight, flight or freeze. In this example, because it involves someone that one loves dearly, for me it is about fighting. It is about saving a life. Every Monday morning, I pick up the phone and work on my business because I get to make a difference in someone's life, and I love what I do. You have a choice too—show up bitter at work, give yourself an excuse to not do your best, spend the extra 20 minutes in bed, and 'not show up'. When you run your own business, it is common to feel that you have the world in your hands, and you just decide not to show up some days. But it is on these days that it becomes even more important for you to raise the necessary urgency; to tell yourself that you are there for a purpose, your business is to serve others and you get to serve through what you do.

6. Practise, practise, practise

Perhaps the one most important trait of building a results-based habit is to keep doing it every day—showing up, not being afraid to fail, and keeping on improving what you do. Think of the phrase, "Insanity is doing the same thing over and over, expecting different results". Well, success also means doing the same thing over and over until you become an undisputed expert in what you do. Good cold callers will pick up the phone and reach out to 40–60 callers a day. After the 100th call, I am confident that they will have found a method that has worked for them, and they'll continue to tweak their messaging to different groups of people that they would have reached. In my earlier example, I practised on the piano 8–12 hours a day, preparing for my exams. It got to the point that, on the day of the exam, I could play with my eyes closed; I knew what I had to do, and I was in autopilot mode. My subconscious mind manifested itself positively. That is the subconscious mind that we need to feed to become unconsciously great at our work. There is just no shortcut to this—just practise, more practise, and even more practise. Part of getting good at what we do is also getting feedback from people we trust. Welcome the feedback, evaluate and continue to improve. Great orators and debaters did not just wing it in their time in the spotlight. It takes hours of practice and understanding the issues that will prepare you for the big day. When I work with a client, it is not just about the hour session or the day-long workshop. It is about understanding their needs; it is taking the time to understand their industries and what they do, researching, connecting with experts, having discovery calls to understand their pain points and challenges. All of this takes time and effort, but it is all worth it because when I get to work with my clients, I absolutely understand how I can add value to them.

Chapter 8 Harnessing your circle of influence

Harmony: Your circle of influence

Starting your own business and being an entrepreneur is about realizing a dream. It could be about bringing an innovation or a product to your customers. It is also about adding value to an existing situation that you see around you. The bigger the problem that you can solve, the bigger your value will be.

As an entrepreneur, you must be knowledgeable in the field that you are in, or at least have the resources that will highlight your business's strength and the areas of focus. To continue staying relevant, you need to consistently and continually invest, both in yourself and your business, know current and future trends and try out different product and service mixes to ensure that you are keeping current. This is undoubtedly a very difficult task, but so is being an entrepreneur. It takes a certain level of tenacity to focus.

It is equally important that your business takes relationships seriously. No business survives on its own. You need suppliers and vendors to provide you with the resources that you need to produce your products/services; you need employees to support you in serving your customers, you need customers to buy your products or services, and you need your family and close friends to support and encourage you as an entrepreneur.

Some relationships have been there since you were born—your parents and siblings and families. Over the course of your life, you continue to develop more relationships—in school, in business, and, of course, as you start your own family. You create relationships as you come across a variety of people over the course of your life. Some will push you forward, some will drag you down and some will stay your lifelong connections. Realize that all the connections you have and will make are part of your journey to success.

If you were to break down your relationships, you would realize that all your connections fall into one of four categories, which we will refer to, unassumingly, as Spheres One, Two, Three and Four as illustrated:

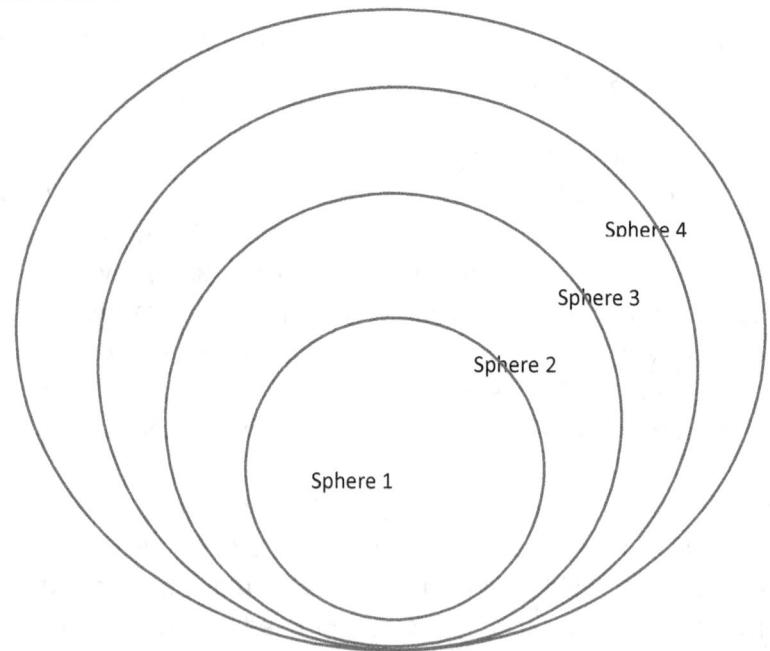

Sphere 1 is the centre of the circle. The relationships that belong in this centre are normally the people who know you at a personal level, and these include your immediate family and possibly some very close friends that have been with you for such a long time they know how to complete your sentences. Many times, these are the people that you would do anything for. These are the people you will continue to stay in touch with even after years of separation. As close as they are to you on a personal level, the people who belong in this circle of influence in your life may not necessarily be the ones that you will depend on to help you realize your goals and your dreams. You may confide in them, but sometimes you may notice them dragging you down. If you are familiar with the book of Job in the Bible, you will realize that Job confided in three of his closest buddies, Eliphaz, Bildad and Zophar. All three of them cared for Job at a personal level and knew what his struggles were, but they were not necessarily the ones who helped him in his time of need. They were there, at times, criticizing his decisions and his actions that resulted in the devastation that Job faced in his life. Your spouse may support you emotionally and provide you with the unconditional love that you need, but he or she may not be the one that understands some of the challenges that you face as an entrepreneur and a business person; not because they don't care— it simply means that they do not understand the issues enough to provide you with the kind of advice or support that you require as an entrepreneur. I share with my wife what I do everyday, and with the people that I meet or have connected with too. As much as she supports what I do emotionally and unconditionally, my wife may not be the one I can go to for advice. Likewise, she may have a friend in which she confides but is outside of the centre sphere. They may even share stories and confide in each other in some personal matters.

Beyond the intimate relationships that you have with immediate family and close buddies, the next sphere of influence is typically made up of people who are there with you when you need them as you build your business and yourself. Think of the people in this sphere as your coach, mentor, counsellor and mastermind groups. Although they may not know you as well as the people in Sphere 1, these are the people that you go to when you have struggles. You know that whatever that is discussed in this sphere stays in this sphere, and you can openly share with them. They are the ones that will help you structure your thinking, encourage you to dream and strategize with you to hold you accountable in realizing the goals that you set for yourself. Personally, I belong to a group that meets weekly; we either read through business and leadership books or help support each other in our areas of need. I have been in this group for several years, and these are the guys that I rely on to share some of the joys and pains of life and business. I know that every member of this group has the best intentions to encourage and coach each other out of any situation. I also work with a coach one-on-one that helps me develop a roadmap that I can work with and holds me accountable for the areas that I said I want to develop. At the end of the day, your goals are yours alone, and you need to take the actions, most times uncomfortable, that will achieve your goals. As much as the people in this sphere can provide you with the support and push you in ways that you need, it is up to you to implement and execute the blueprints and build them from the ground up to see the success that you want and desire.

Sphere 3 typically consists of your relationships with business associates, suppliers, clients, networking groups, friends, and extended relatives. You have an established relationship with these folks, but they may not necessarily be the ones that you go to for advice or help in reaching your goals. Their interactions with you typically stop at either the social or business level and may not go further than that. These may be colleagues, people you do business with, or some of your social friends. You don't necessarily share your life stories with them. Sometimes they're fun to hang out with or to do business with, but that is the extent.

The fourth and final sphere are people that are toxic to your relationships or serve no purpose to even be considered in your circle of influence. They are negative influences and continuously find faults in the things that you do. All of us know several people we would categorize in this category. Sometimes we hang on to these relationships because of sentimental or historical reasons but, honestly, if it continues to be stressful and detrimental to your well-being and success, these people should be eliminated from your circle of influence.

The examples given in the spheres of influence are merely guidelines. There is no hard and fast rule to determine who belongs in which sphere. As well, people can shift from one sphere to the next or have both feet in adjoining spheres. For example, I have known spouses who work really well together in running their businesses. They are able to overcome all challenges together and have been there for each other throughout the time that they spent in the business. I work with a business partner where we continually challenge each other to work on business together. We rely on each other for support and encouragement.

As you evaluate your relationships and as you go through your contact lists, one thing you can do to start this process is segment your relationships. Are there people that you thought would belong in a certain sphere that should not be there? How difficult would it be to shift a person from one sphere to another? Who are you letting into your spheres? Should they be there? Why or why not?

Why aren't you more influential?

A very common reason that many people are not influential is that they think influence is something that comes with their position or who they are. That's what I used to think. Well, because I am a father, my son should know that I have influence. That worked for a few years, and then I realized that this belief is not sustainable. It may also be that, because I am your employer or your boss, I should have influence in telling you what you need to do. That was the case more than 50 years ago, when we had a society of do-ers and not as many thinkers—the industrial revolution and the educational system prepared us to be good do-ers of work and not thinkers of work. Influencing, unfortunately, is not something that will come when you want it to or be based on who you are. It takes effort and planning. Think of your last interview for a job. Did you just go and 'wing it'? You likely researched the organization and its structure, what they do, what their strategic plan is, who you're interviewing with and their background, how your experiences will fit with what they are looking for, outlining your strength and weaknesses, and many more items that are potential questions. In your big moment in the interview, you had planned what to say to influence the interviewers into believing you are the best person for the job. You took the time and the effort to plan for big events such as these, but you forget that influence is an "always-on" phenomenon. You do not become a saviour or a hero today while you were behaving like a mean person the day before. You're always observed—your actions and your words. It is not a 'moment' but can sometimes take years of practice.

Building powerful and high-trust relationships

As an entrepreneur and value creator, you need to build 'power relationships'. Power relationships are probably more important to a business than all the money in the world. Imagine having the ability to pick up the phone and call someone of high influence, like the President or Prime Minister, for a favour or to get something done. I am sure that you would be more interested in having this type of relationship than $100,000, but I personally would not mind having both.

So, what does it take to build these powerful, high-trust relationships? It all starts and ends with trust. Trust is foundational. Your business will not succeed, and you will not succeed in life, if you are untrustworthy. It is the core of any relationship. The ability to build a high-trust relationship means that you will do what you say you will do when you say you will do it, and you'll do it well and be proactive. It takes effort and hard work to build trust. Think of a person whom you would trust unconditionally. What makes that person so trustworthy? Is it because of the person's position or his vocation, or is it the way he conducts himself? What about a business? Have you ever had a bad experience with a business and vowed to never, for the rest of your life, have any connection with that business? What did they do or not do to earn your wrath? I have come up with five simple steps that you can begin to use to build a powerful, high-trust relationship.

Connect on a personal level: One powerful way to build trust in your relationships is to find out what makes the other person tick. What motivates the other person? It is about understanding what they need and then being able to fulfill that need. It is also about letting your own guard down and being vulnerable to exposure. If you have a conflict with your spouse because your spouse isn't doing what you want them to do, you have to get it into your head that it may not be that they are lazy and disrespecting you. Maybe it is your identity and your motivation that is not aligned with them. In my household, I am typically the one that does the cleaning and cooking. I would sometimes get upset when I am out on a long day and come home to a dirty house that is not vacuumed or mopped. Is that justified? If I told my wife, "You always leave the house full of crumbs", or "You never vacuum the floor", or "I give up talking to you and will just do it myself", I am putting a guard up and not allowing for further conversations on the topic. That's indignation and it does not make you more influential. We have to get to the point where influencing is not about me but the other person.

Perhaps she is not aligned to what my inner desire is—to have order and cleanliness. It isn't so much about the act of vacuuming, but the understanding of a specific need and identity.

Tell the truth: Being in business means you have to be vulnerable to admit wrong when it is wrong, instead of passing the buck or coming up with excuses. You probably have witnessed a leader of a country throwing some of his/her cabinet members under the bus for comments made that are not in line with 'public opinion'. Well, the buck stops at the top; when this 'house-cleaning' happens, the leader is not being accountable for actions that his team has made. The leader himself loses trust, in this example, because the action of one reflects the entire government. This can very well relate to a business, too. It takes courage to be vulnerable in front of customers, staff and other stakeholders.

Overdeliver: Another way to start building trust is to provide an excellent and amazing experience for your stakeholders. It does not have to be a customer. If you want to build a high-trust and powerful relationship, you have to show that you are worthy of one. Go beyond expectations and be the person that you would like to hang out with and trust. That could be in the form of service, knowledge in a certain area or just knowing where to go to find solutions to a problem.

Be Prompt: I can't stress this enough. Return phone calls and emails. Or faxes if you are still into that. It happens so often—many business owners undermine the importance of being responsive. Do not take anyone for granted, even the people who are in your inner circle. It could even mean paying your bills promptly and not waiting to be asked. If you cannot be trusted with a little, you cannot be trusted with a lot. Have you ever sent an email to someone asking for information, only to never receive a call back or a response? How did that make you feel? This goes to being respectful of people's time and effort and treating others as you want to be treated.

Be Consistent: Have you ever had a boss who changed his mind every once in a while? Or has said one thing to you but claimed that it was never said or was interpreted wrongly? Or provided preferential treatment openly with your customers? These are examples of inconsistency, and that is the bane of all businesses. Being true to your word, and practising them consistently every day, will show others that there are no surprises, and you mean what you say when you say it.

Differentiate: How are you different from the people that offer similar products or services? What you need is to be distinctive. In order to build a high-trust relationship, you need to differentiate yourself from the crowd. For years, we have been trained to blend into the environment and show our clients "best practices". There's nothing wrong with best practices when it matters, but best practices sometimes mean copying from others. Copy what's right and what you should, but are you copying so much that you blend into the crowd? How will you get noticed?

Be Flexible: There are times when there will be disagreements, whether it's with your business partner, a client or others. In this instance, you need to be flexible to identify a possible third solution to a problem instead of playing the blame game. Far too common in the society that we live in is that it's never our problem. If you are to build a powerful, high-trust relationship, it is critical that you be flexible and able to be patient, calm and able to solve a problem in a civil way. Your ability to read situations, be truthful, honest and flexible but firm can earn you points as being a person who is trustworthy.

Reflection

1. Think of your own circle of connections that are closest to you (family, friends, professional connections, etc.)
   A. Sort your contacts into the four relationship spheres.
   B. How do you increase your connections in relationship spheres 1 and 2?
   C. Are you spending too much time with people you regard as negative or toxic?

2. Having a peer support group is a vital component in practising and harnessing your influencing potential. Many times, it can be your spouse, a mentor, a coach, even a therapist. Remember, influencing is a two-way process, and it takes time, energy and strategy. Is there a group, mastermind, coach or anyone that you can connect with—one you can be authentic with?

Chapter 9 Gaining breakthroughs in selling

The word "sales" itself scares many people. Sometimes, it is still a scary word to me. If you are a business owner or an entrepreneur, guess what—you need to sell what you have or you won't have the opportunity to do what you love.

It is one of the essential skills that we all need and have been practising since we were little. When one parent refuses to say "Yes" to a child asking for candy, the child will automatically approach the other parent to get what he wants. That can be considered one component of sales—keep approaching a prospect with different tactics until you get to an ultimate decision-maker. When you are interviewing for your first job, you are selling your skills to an organization who will 'buy' your talent and offer you a job. When you are interested in a potential mate, you may go all out to look your best before you go on your first date so that he or she will have a good impression of you. All of this is selling.

When I was working in a large consulting firm, we had targets to achieve. I loved the consulting part of the work, but I didn't enjoy the sales part of it—attending mixers, networking events, following up with contacts, taking people out for drinks and dinner, football games, and, ultimately, making and closing the next sales calls. All of this was just not who I am. But I also know that if I am not *selling* more consulting work, I can't *do* any consulting work. I prefer to spend countless hours perfecting the perfect proposal in response to a 'Request-For-Proposal', but then the success rates for such tenders are usually quite low. There is only so much that the partners or the higher-ups can sell. Everyone on the totem pole has a role in the sales process.

After I started my own business, I was in a do-or-die situation. I had to go out and reach out to prospects, either making cold (and some warm) calls, sharing with them what my new business venture is, asking for a sale or a referral and ensuring that there was sufficient follow-up. This was a totally new space for me to venture, one that I was absolutely uncomfortable with, and probably miles away from my comfort zone. I don't have a problem speaking to a crowd or spending hours talking someone that I know, but tell me that I need to make a sale, and I would probably scurry away into my cave. I had to change my mindset in a hard way. I needed to tell myself that 'sales' is not a bad word. In the Priority Management world, we see ourselves as problem-solvers and relationship builders. In every outreach I make, I consider myself as helping another person or organization in need of getting a problem solved. Through me. Once I switched this mindset, selling itself took a different turn because I am out there solving a problem and forming a new relationship. If your initial intention was to make a quick buck, then for you, sales are probably not much different from the high-pressure sales tactics like timeshares employ to get you to make a decision 'right now' while the offer is still valid.

I can write an entire book about selling, and it is not the intention of this chapter to go through all the elements about sales. There are a lot of great literature and programs that speak to selling effectively. It is more about how selling and owning a business is something that we cannot avoid and have to embrace.

In this chapter, I will focus on a few key points in selling products and services that I believe are essential for any business owner and entrepreneur to thrive.

Developing relationships to solve a problem

We all like to buy, but we do not like to be sold to. It's just our nature. If I feel pressured to make a sales decision, however good the offer is, I will most likely think twice. If I have to make a decision in the next five minutes before an offer disappears forever, I will probably let it disappear forever. If I see a salesperson in a department store running towards me the moment I walk into a store and starting to tail me around, I probably will walk away. But if that sales associate from the dealership offers to let me have the car for a week and offers to drive me around while I have my car fixed, the pressure of buying is reduced, and I am more inclined to 'work with him' to come up with a deal. These are probably in their sales tactics that many dealerships offer in building relationships with prospects.

In many tourist places across the world, you may see rows and rows of shops selling souvenirs. Most of what they all sell are the same. They probably came from the same suppliers. The same t-shirts, candles, cookies and coffee table books. As business owners, they need to move beyond same-ness. Although they are all selling similar things, sometimes it is the personal connection that you make with one of the staff that makes all the difference. Perhaps it is a staff member that was able to strike up a conversation that resonated with you, or you had asked a question about where the nearest bathroom is, and you continued to connect at that level. These conversations may or may not be intentional, but you were communicating on the same wavelength. You formed a relationship, and the salesperson solved a problem that you had—direction to a bathroom. Maybe there isn't a washroom nearby, but they were able to let you use their staff washroom. They went above and beyond to serve a need that you have. Notice the difference between this and the high-pressure timeshare salesperson?

It's not any different from what *you* sell. What is it that you offer that stands out from the rest? This is a tough question that some people find hard to answer. You have built up your life to where it is today because of experiences that only you have lived through. In my first sessions as a facilitator, I tried to follow the facilitator guide almost to a tee, and I probably lost that client forever because I was reading more than I was relating to the participants. I learned through that experience, and after familiarizing myself with the content through practice, practice and more practice, when the material became second nature, I was able to relate more of my personal experiences to the program; that resonates more with participants. It is not different from selling. It is about understanding your prospect's needs and tailoring a solution to meet that need. Whether you are selling a product, a food, or a service, it is critical that you understand the market and who you are serving. Sales is a targeted process, but know that somewhere out there, someone needs what you have. You just have to go look for them.

Part of building a relationship is to be sure that you know what you are selling and confident in the products or services that you represent. When I am selling my learning and development solutions, I focus on the provincial market of Saskatchewan. The people I want to engage with are decision-makers in organizations that want to make a difference by introducing better and more efficient ways to work, in order to reduce stress and increase organizational efficiency and profitability. Out of the roughly 37 million population of Canada, and about 1 million in the province of Saskatchewan, my target is among approximately 4,000 decision-makers across the province. That narrows down my market and makes it much easier to develop the correct messages for the right people.

Consider your business, and try to answer these questions, in as much detail as possible, about the ideal client that will use your products and services:

- What is the demography of your ideal client (examples include age range, gender, education, marital status, occupation, income)?
- What is their lifestyle?
- What are their aspirations and goals?
- What are their beliefs and opinions?
- What do they value?
- What are their fears and challenges?
- Where do they 'hang out' (virtually or physically)?
- What is the lifetime value of the client?
- How much would they be willing to spend on your products and services?

Once you have successfully created this profile for your ideal client, also known as the avatar, you can then map out your client journey or client experience; imagine yourself as the ideal client, working with you from introduction to signing off on a sale and coming back as a repeat client or as a referral source.

Developing the skills to solve a problem

Part of being able to present yourself as a brand means you need to develop your brand. What do you stand for? When people see you, what do they see? How do you show up?

I have a client who refers to me as 'the productivity guy' because of the work I do in teaching people to be more effective in what *they* do. It is a brand that I have created—a person who can help clients with their priority management and entrepreneurship endeavours.

There really is no question about this. You have to be good at what you do in order to sell what you have. This is not something a coach can help you with. Even if you are not good in this particular area, you need to be well informed about the industry to know what needs to be done to be good at it. One of the businesses I run is a day spa. Am I the one doing the services? Gosh, no. But I understand enough of the industry, the available treatments, the latest available tech and research that goes into the different treatment types, and the necessary building of trust with employees and clients that we are delivering the best services, using the best products, delivering the best results for them in their health and wellness routines. Using these same ideas, I have helped others in the industry to develop the necessary operational and business skills to build their business.

Part of having the skills is also telling your story. Personalize the stories and engage with your customers. You may have seen or experienced some restaurants that are just oozing with their owner's story. Some clients will gravitate to that because it resonates with them. These may include the owner's passion for local ingredients, their passion for certain foods and cooking styles, their own lifestyle, and others. Or they will approach a speaker and author who is able to use their own life experiences to impart knowledge to their clients, sometimes in humorous and comical ways.

Develop a consistent selling system

Consistency is the key to success. The more you practise and the more you do, the better you will get. But you need a framework and a process that you use consistently to allow you to know what you do. You can't measure success if you do not know what you are measuring and how you are measuring it. Let's look at this framework of sales developed by Priority Management in the Selling Breakthroughs program:

Need: The first thing you need to identify is what the client needs. It is so important that we establish what it is that your prospect wants. This is where you need to ask the right questions to understand what the problems are that you can solve for a client. I remember one of my first conversations with a prospect. After some small talk, I began to tell the prospect that I can help him make a lot of money when he works with me. Wow, was I put in my place in no time. He responded to me, "How do you know that I don't make enough?" Of course, I lost that trust with him, and I've never seen him since. It is critical in needs assessment that we also build a high level of trust with a prospect so they know that we can help them with the challenges they face. Part of identifying the need is also to ensure that we apply the right influencing skills necessary to extract the right information that we need to formulate our solution.

Priority: I am sure you have experienced salespeople telling you all the features of a product that will benefit you, but you find that none of the features actually benefit you or are something that you particularly want or desire. I had the opportunity to work with several community-based organizations whose role was to build up its membership base. The leadership of these organizations would create collaboration with businesses that provide benefits to members. These may have included special pricing on products and services. In their conversations with potential and existing members, one of the first things that was shared was the benefits of becoming a member of their organization, and their first talking points would be the discounts that they would enjoy with various businesses. Well, needless to say, there wasn't much take-up on the membership. One thing that was lacking in these conversations is the surfacing of the motives of the 'buyer'. What is it that the buyer is looking for? The Selling Breakthroughs model from Priority Management highlights that effective selling means you need to understand the motives from your prospect's viewpoint—does it do the task that is required, does it represent value to the client, and does it satisfy a feeling? Remember, people respond because something connects with them at an emotional level. They may become a member of a community-based organization because the cause that they fight for resonates with them; maybe because it has impacted them at some point. People buy a particular car because the design and features resonate with them and they are able to see themselves in it, having experienced the 'feeling' of being behind the wheel of that particular model of vehicle.

Solution and Implementation: I mentioned that the bigger the problem that you can solve, the bigger your value will be. The higher the value of your services, the better you are at growing your business. Value is nothing but what someone thinks your service or product is worth. Why does a buyer willingly buy something that cost twice as much as the product next to it that has pretty much the same function? It is the perceived value. Many would rather wait to see their family doctor rather than have a registered nurse work with them, although the registered nurse would know just as much about common illnesses as a doctor. In a church, many people would rather the Lead Pastor pray for them compared to other people, because there is a perception that the Lead Pastor is more 'powerful' in that regard.

Sometimes, to create that value you need to create a demand, and that demand could come in various forms. What is the problem that you have a solution for? Many entrepreneurs are extremely knowledgeable in what they do and what they have to offer but are unable to translate that knowledge and passion into sales. A simple way out for many is to keep trying different things. Well, the more things you try, the more diluted your 'brand' will be, and the more you are diluted, the less focused your service or product becomes. Ultimately, you may have trouble branding yourself. You turn into a jack-of-all-trades. It may work for some, but for many, that is a huge challenge.

Relationship: Sales is about building a strong, powerful, high-trust relationship with a buyer. That is first and foremost. Then it is about solving a problem. No one wants to buy from a sleazy salesperson. Here is where it becomes so important to relate to the buyer. It is all about them, their motivation, their desires, and how you are able to meet their demands. This is where it may also mean that you disqualify clients. There is no way that you are not going to hear a "No" in your role as an entrepreneur. If you continue to be stuck at a "No", then you aren't likely to go very far. You need to be able to discriminate and disqualify clients. Not everyone will be your client. But the ones who are, treat them well, give them the best service that you can, and maintain that relationship. Sustaining is a crucial element of relationships. Many of my clients who previously had done some work with me are now my friends, and they know where to go when they need help. Or they can refer their friends and colleagues to me when they see a need.

Develop a network of support

We live in an age where we are all dependent on each other. No one lives on an island, and we all have a set of specific skills that we are able to offer the world. As a consultant and entrepreneur who helps other entrepreneurs and businesses, I have the skills to help clients visualize their future, set goals and develop pathways that set the trajectories of success. I need a network of support that will help me, as well as my clients, with other areas. Although I know the strategies to market and brand, I am not the one you turn to when it's time to build a website or develop social media content. Nor am I the person who can give you detailed advice on legal, taxation or investment matters. But I have built a team and a network of experts in various fields whom I turn to for help, and this network is also one I surround myself with and can turn to—to help my clients build their business with sound advice and implementation.

Many of you who are new to starting a business will have a tendency to worry about the cost of hiring help; hence, you tend to do it on your own. You think that you do not have the extra few dollars to have someone keep your books up to date, or hire an accountant help you file your year-ends, or get someone to support you in building your social media strategy to help you sell more of what you sell. What if you shifted your thinking to "Can I afford not to"? If hiring a bookkeeper for $50 per hour is too much, perhaps think of it this way: It frees you up to do the work that you are more worthy of. Perhaps you have calculated your own hourly cost (what it should be). While focusing your efforts on doing the higher-leveraged activities, is it not worth it to farm out or delegate the activities that someone else can do better?

I have been in your shoes. I have tried to keep my books and expenses up to date, and I have failed miserably. At one point, I was owing the government a lot of unpaid taxes because my books weren't up to date and my taxes weren't done on time. I've received letters from tax collectors, my utility bills weren't paid, invoices were not sent out on time, and the list goes on. I was exposed to a lot of risks. These are the things that every entrepreneur needs to consider. We need to accept the reality that it's not just about doing what you love. By leveraging on external help, we are not only helping ourselves but helping our business grow in our blindspots. It's about knowing what we don't know, and needing someone else to tell us that.

Develop a well-oiled automation process

How do you currently generate leads? For a long time, we have been taught that developing one-on-one relationships, getting referrals and positive reviews from clients and a one-size-fits-all email marketing campaign is the way to go.

Selling in the 21st century has evolved, and it has evolved exponentially since 2020 because people needed new ways of reaching out to customers. Although traditional selling still works, (very effectively, I may say, in some markets), entrepreneurs need to start thinking about automation with the lead generation process. Data is your friend, and the more you have, the more audience you will reach. Ever noticed the "cookie permission" that so many websites are now asking you for? I would guess that a majority of people would not hesitate to think before clicking "agree to all" so that your experiences can be tailored. Not many realize that some sites also mention sending your information to their partners to enhance your browsing experience! Data is money, if you use it properly. Build up your database of clients because this is where you will continue to grow your client base. Email marketing is dead, they say, but it is still one of the most successful tools there are, if done right. It's not about sending a one-size-fits-all email to all and sundry and hoping that at least a couple might stick. This form of lead generation has taken on a very sophisticated turn that, if done right, augments customers on their specific needs, and takes the time out of your high-leverage activity-filled day to generate more positive leads.

There are opportunities for you to automate many of the lead generation processes that continue your work to engage with current, past and future clients through intelligent automation. With a proper strategy towards automation, you can be sure to continue keeping up to date with your clients with the most current content, and they will continue to keep you top of mind whenever your services or products are required.

Reflection
1. o you currently have a sales process? How do you measure your sales successes?
2. The world has 7 billion people. You can't sell everything to everyone. If you think of what you *can* provide, what will you sell? Who are your target markets?

3. You are skilled at what you do, and you have a product and/or a service that your customers desire. But have you thought about your network of support that will help you with areas that you are unskilled at? Or perhaps there are some areas that are better delegated to others?
4. Have you considered what parts of your business can be automated? Think of the following triggers:
    i. Highly targeted emails to specific types of clients that look at their behaviour, needs and wants
    ii. Sending email (or text where appropriate) notifications at various points of contact—welcome email, when an invoice is sent or paid, when a call-to-action is received, whe an appointment is made and confirmed, when a quote is sent, about abandoned shopping cart, etc.
    iii. Follow-up text or emails to clients or respondents to your messages or newsletters
    iv. Subscription renewals and reminders
    v. Timed follow-ups via email or text messages

Are there any other triggers that you could have automated to ensure that your clients continue to be engaged? How will this save you time and increase your touch points with your clients, present and future?

Chapter 10 Making impactful decisions

Every action that we take, every day, is a choice that we make. From the most mundane of events – like what time you should go to bed, what will you eat for breakfast, and how many cups of coffee should you consume – to business decisions such as where you should rent your office space, should you have another drink, should you drive home after having that extra drink, what services will you offer and how you will serve your customers. The words that you say to another person are also a choice that you make. Whether or not you pick up the dirty laundry and put the toilet seat up/down are also choices.

Being busy is also a choice. I said it—being busy is a choice that you make. In my productivity and time management workshops, I tell clients to stop using the phrase "I'm busy". In today's world, it's almost a rite of passage that you need to be in a state of busyness to stay important. Busy doing something just means something else isn't as important to you right at that moment. When you are busy, it just means that you have not taken the time or the effort to plan prior to execution. Of course, I do get it that stuff gets in the way sometimes, like the car breaks down and you lost two hours of productivity, or the school called for you to pick up your son, who just scraped his knee. These things do happen, and I am not discounting that, but proper plans allow for flexibility to accommodate emergencies and changes. Your day will be planned whether or not you like it; it just depends on whether you are the one planning it and making decisions that impact the plan.

Your decision affects people around you

We do not live alone in this world. Every action that we take and the choices that we make impact another person. If you are a parent, your actions and words are continuously observed by your child. All of us have, at some point in our parenting life, seen our kids emulating a behaviour or choice of words that we have used that we are not entirely proud of. I know I have, and I'm always completely horrified when those words or actions are repeated back at me at the most inopportune time. There have been many occasions where I've also been very pleasantly surprised when my sons demonstrate the good behaviours that I believe I have instilled through them through my actions and choices that I make.

Likewise, every decision that you make will impact your business. What type of business you should be in, every call that you make, your marketing strategies, the training that you will take, the kinds of people that you will hire, the types of clients that you target—all these will affect your business.

Passion affects your decisions

You've heard me talk about passion and how some people are just so motivated about it. Well, passion itself is a big reason why someone would want to be in business for themselves. It's because they see a void in the marketplace that they can fill. That itself is a decision. Getting into business and being a business owner or entrepreneur itself is a big decision that will affect you and those closest to you. It is a lifestyle; it is not a job that you go to and then forget about when you leave work. Owning your own business and being an entrepreneur is a lifestyle that you should learn to embrace if you are planning to be in for the long haul. I have worked with many people who are in business just because they did not like to report to someone else. That is a good reason and an option for sure. Many of them will turn to business ownership as a career—starting something new or buying a franchise or the like. Some may thrive at the business for a few years.

If you are in the business because you do not like the idea of reporting to another person, you need to go back to the drawing board and really start identifying where your passion really is. Your passion is what drives you to grow and succeed in the business. I have worked with successful men who own beauty salons and spas. They are passionate about the industry but may not necessarily be the ones working on their clients. Their passion can be infectious, and employees and clients will see that through their business, the way their employees interact with the customers, the kinds of posting that they see on social media, and just the energy that exudes from their passion. Clint, the owner of a furnace and duct cleaning business, said that he did not grow up wanting to own a duct-cleaning business (which kid did?) As his career progressed, he saw an opportunity in the market, and he seized it. His passion for his business grew from there, and that passion has turned into a success story for him and his family. Now his son may one day grow up wanting to take over for his dad and be a duct-cleaner, or at the very least, own a duct cleaning business.

Your decision affects your business

Business leaders and entrepreneurs make decisions all the time. During the pandemic, Clint made the decision to not sit still but rather ensure that he is taking the necessary steps to keep his employees and his clients safe. By keeping up to date with the latest news, regulations and government recommendations, he started putting in place additional checks, increasing the frequency of the sanitizing of his equipment, and ensuring that the clients that he works with are also aware of the additional precaution that his business is taking. All of these extra measures ensured that the service that his company delivers was still among the best in the business, while keeping everyone safe and protected to the extent that he is able to. He made the decision to keep his prices the same, even with the increased cost of doing business. As a leader, he also made the decision to keep the business going by reflecting on some internal processes that he had always wanted to review and improve; in the process, he renegotiated the costs of his supplies, invested in his employees and grew his workforce. How will these decisions affect his business in the long run? It is anybody's guess, but from my vantage point, he is well prepared to scale his business to the next level once the pandemic is over. While other businesses will start to pick up from where they left off, he is well on his way to growth. Could it backfire? Nothing is foolproof. Markets could dynamically change, there may be second or third lockdowns, his supply chain may be severely affected, and costs may go up. There are countless other reasons why his decisions won't work. But it's a choice that was made, and a risk that he was willing to chance after taking into account the pros and cons. It boils down to his willingness to take on that risk.

Making decisions while looking at competing interests

Many entrepreneurs that I know, including me, are always grappling with competing interests that want a piece of you. Since becoming a business owner, I have had contacts come up to me, wanting me to be a member of their network marketing business. I must decide whether the business is aligned with what I do and how I want to be known. I have decided that although I like some of the products sold through this channel, I will not be in the recruiting of the business. It is not what I want to be known for. Another competing interest that I catch myself in is whether to spend an extra hour on the business or spend the time with my sons. Most entrepreneurs and business owners are the same, or at least similar. You need to find a balance and integration between spending precious time with your spouse and kids, running the business (and in some cases, multiple businesses), making sure that you are continuously developing yourself and your team and growing the business. What do the balance and the trade-off look like? If you don't have your kids for a few days, or a couple of weekends a month, is that a trade-off? It is not up to me to answer that question, because balance is different from one person (or family) to another. Most of us will know, or at least have heard of, the local restaurant run by an immigrant family that is on the job every day of the week, and sometimes the kids join in working in the business as well. That's the choice and decisions that they made. How does it affect their family relationships? I have heard different results. Some of these kids grow up having the same work ethic as their hardworking parents and carving successful lives for themselves, while others went the other way because they lacked familial love growing up. It all comes down to whether there is harmony of work, marriage, family and your personal lives.

During the pandemic, many business owners were looking at their business and wondering whether they should invest in technology during a time when sales are down. All of these are interests that seem to be polar opposites. A few common questions that I have seen are, "How can I afford the extra steps that are needed to run my business?" or "How will I afford to hire a coach to help me shift my business or the technology required to keep the business running?" These are hard questions, and only you can decide what is best for the situation. The risk to these additional investments at difficult times is, of course, that it does not work, and we may have to pile on more debt. On the other hand, what if it does work, and you missed the boat?

Thinking in the moment

Many of you reading this book are so focused on what's in front of you and focused in the moment that you have lost the ability to think. We want things in an instant. Information is available to us in an instant. There's definitely a reality to the term "men simply don't think", and this is not meant to be gender specific. The average worker today gets to work on a Monday morning focused on how to get through the week as quickly and as painlessly as possible, and hopefully they'll have enough money for beers on Friday and Saturday. That's the painful reality today. What better options are there? Make a decision to love Mondays. I love Monday mornings. I get to have another week to make a difference to another person or business that I touch. That's definitely an option worth exploring. You make the decision to love your job or to hate it. You may be in a job that you have no desire or passion for. Make the decision to perform your best in it anyway. If you can't, then make the decision to find another job or, better still, to create your own job.

Do I have the option to consider selling my company and returning to a regular and stable job? Sure, I do. Do I want that option? I choose not to and continue to want to grow my business. The options and decisions that you consider are based on what you want. Everything that happens in your life is based on the decisions that you make. You have no excuses. As much as some of us want to blame our upbringing, the opportunities that were presented, the economy, our family, and even where we are, we make the decision to stay where we are, not make excuses or make the irrevocable decision to advance. These are choices that you must make, not anyone else.

Decisions are based on emotions

One area that we do not normally look at is how many of our decisions are based on emotions. People buy because they can connect emotionally to a service, product, or person. Walk into a car dealership, and unless you ask for it no one in the dealership will tell you the technical specifications of a vehicle you are looking at. What they will tell you is how it feels to be in the driver's seat. The exhilaration of reaching 100km/h in 4.2s. How sexy the car looks as it approaches you. How it captures other people's attention. The ambience and feeling of comfort in the cabin. You might also take the car back for a weekend to experience it yourself. Once you are emotionally connected to the car, it's hard for you to return the keys. Remember, you had walked into the dealership and had told your spouse and the sales representative that, "We are just looking".

You may come up with a list of advantages, disadvantages, wants, needs, affordability, and many other factors, but when it's crunch time, it's our emotional state that sometimes skews our decision-making process.

There are times in your life when peace trumps logic in decisions. For a business leader, sometimes there is an inner voice that speaks to you in making decisions, and sometimes the inner voice may defy logic. Christians may attribute this inner voice as the Holy Spirit. That said, these inner voices may need to pass through several 'tests' before you can affirm that there is peace in your heart while you make decisions. These are the times that you might have to go with the gut feel—also knowing that this gut feel is a risk all on its own. For my duct cleaner friend, all analysis pointed to him not being able to afford to expand his workforce, but he went with his gut feel this was an opportunity for him.

I personally believe that the inner voice and the peace are provided by the Holy Spirit. You may believe in another entity that drives your decision-making process. Of course, this inner voice has to align with your personal goals and vision for yourself and for your business, as well as support your belief system and values.

Factors that influence the decision-making process for business owners and entrepreneurs

As a business owner or as an entrepreneur, you need to find a balance between logic and peace. Hindsight is always 20/20. You may have the epiphany of why something didn't make sense, but you did it anyway (or didn't do it), and it becomes clear at the end. It definitely takes a level of gutsiness to make some decisions. As you are making decisions, think of several factors:

- How will my decision impact others? Who will be impacted, and how will they be impacted by it?
- What factors do I need to consider when making decisions? These could range from life experiences, level of commitment and desired outcomes, personal preferences, market preferences, personal beliefs, and even cognitive biases.
- Which of your decisions are irrevocable? How will you manage irrevocable decisions when things go awry?
- How quickly are you able to bounce back if you made the wrong decision? What would be the impact of the decisions (who is impacted, how will you be impacted)?

Reflection

1. Has there been a time in your life when you made a wrong decision? How did the decision come about? Do you see yourself making the same mistake again?
2. What is the next upcoming decision that you need to make? Perhaps it is as simple as deciding that you will write a daily journal, start a business, or pivot your business. What are the steps that you will take now to ensure that you have considered all aspects of the decision?

Chapter 11 Impediments to success

Knowing where you want to go is the first step. The previous two chapters highlighted some ways that you can take to set yourself up for success. But the road to success isn't always smooth. Along the way, you will need to make detours, take a few steps back, earn some scars, and perhaps even change gears and move in a different direction. The COVID-19 pandemic had an impact that caused so many businesses and organizations to change gears on how their business is run and whether or not it is still viable. Many won't survive. That's just the reality of the situation.

However, there are still many things that we can control to stay relevant and be focused on the end state that we desire. We just need to understand some of the common impediments that we continuously face in the world that we live in.

Distractions

Let's explore "a day in the life of *[insert your name]*". Start by looking at the table that you completed in Chapter 2. Calculate the actual productive hours that you had. Do you think you can put in more hours into the day? Have you ever caught yourself in a situation when you were busy every day, but not quite sure about what you have achieved? Take stock of what you were "busy" with. When I am teaching productivity principles, I usually tell my students to avoid using the word 'busy' when describing their day. It simply just means that one thing is more important to you than the other. 'Busy' is a decision that you make. You made the conscious decision to do one task instead of another.

Take, for instance, if you need to drive your child to soccer practice on Wednesdays at 4:00pm. I am sure that you will plan your day around that to ensure that you can leave the office a little earlier so that he or she gets to the practice on time. It's all a matter of perspective. You tend to be more focused and less distracted when you are working 'under pressure'—in this example, leaving work earlier than you normally would.

Another factor to consider when we look at distraction is the idea of being proactive rather than reactive. This idea for achieving success, although it has been around a while, was made famous when Stephen Covey catapulted "Be Proactive" as the Number One habit in his *7 Habits of Highly Effective People*. So why is it so difficult for us to be proactive in the first place?

One of the biggest impediments to being proactive today is the number of distractions that are all around us. It is no surprise that we are a 'reactive' society. We react to the email that arrives in our Inbox, the phone ringing, watching a chef cook the perfect steak or pasta, the allure of finding out the top 10 beaches in the world while you were catching up on the latest sports stat online. You might be doing all this while also responding to text messages that came to you via three other channels and responding to your client's email. All at the same time, or so we think. In this digitally connected world, we are distracted, on average, every eight minutes. For each of these interruptions, it will take us about 15 minutes to resume the interrupted activity at the desired productive level. More so when we find people having to share their home office with kids who stayed home during the course of the pandemic. No wonder we don't get anything done!

It is very important that you understand what some of your common distractions are. List the ten distractions that you constantly face in your everyday life.

My top 10 distractions	How I can overcome them
1.	
2.	
3.	
4.	
5.	
6.	
7.	
8.	
9.	
10.	

Ask yourself this question: *Are these distractions important enough to take away my attention on something that is valuable to me?* I know it is nearly impossible to eliminate all of the distractions, but if you can reduce them or control what you 'allow' to distract you, what will the result be? How will your life change? On the flipside, what is the consequence if you continue getting your life interrupted?

Procrastination

Countless books have been written about procrastination. We all procrastinate. There is countless research about procrastination. The purpose here is not to rehash some of the literature that has been written about it. My purpose is to highlight that it is an impediment to your success, and to make you aware that you can overcome procrastination.

There are many tools in the toolbox of procrastination. We will start exploring why some do whatever it takes and why some find reasons to justify why they are unable to accomplish something or anything at all! Let's start by looking at four of the tools in the toolbox for justifying procrastination.

- *Fear*

If you were to ask anyone you know about failure, I am pretty sure that no one would say they want to fail. None of us deliberately tries to get a failing grade at Math, and we don't deliberately run a business into the ground. We sometimes sugar-coat failure to make it look good in front of others. But fear is one of the tools in the toolbox that justifies procrastination. The fear of failure contributes to procrastination. You'd rather not take that step because you fear that it will fail you.

You may be one of those people who had dreamed of having their own business while growing up in school. You had big hairy audacious goals to be the next big thing. Somewhere along the way, you conformed to society, you found yourself a job and it paid you twice a month with benefits, pension and insurance. You knew what to expect in getting paid and committed yourself to a new shiny car and a mortgage. You were comfortable. You felt security. Suddenly, that dream of yours from a few years back became a distant dream because *What if I gave all of what I have to start my business, and failed?* That thought is too scary for you, so you continue with your current job that you complain about daily. You look forward to Fridays every Monday, and dread Sundays because Monday is just around the corner.

Perhaps you were assigned a big project to work on but didn't know how or where to start. The fear of doing the wrong thing earned this project a corner of your desk. You continue to think about it, but you never got around to work on it because you feared that it wasn't going to turn out the way you imagine it would, and, well, you had no clue where it would end up.

- **Unwillingness**

Sometimes, we just find ourselves unwilling to do and complete a task. It's not that you can't do the work or fear the work; you are just unwilling to do it because it is uninteresting, mundane or you just feel plain lazy! There just isn't a justifiable excuse for unwillingness other that choosing to live in the Now.

I must admit—while I was working in an organization, one of the things that I dreaded doing was keeping my receipts and putting in the monthly claims. There was just something about it that I dreaded. It's a simple exercise, put the claims in, whether it is meals with clients, travels or memberships, and the company reimburses me for what I spent. It was money back for me, but I didn't like doing it. I had no excuse for not doing it, but it just is. So, I put it off until the last minute. There were several times that I missed the deadline and never got reimbursed.

Take stock. Are there some things that you continually procrastinate on just because you are unwilling to do that task? What might that be?

- **Lack of Motivation**

Sometimes, procrastination happens because we are simply unmotivated. It is one of the tools in the toolbox that you have to understand. Sometimes you may be unmotivated because you have a bad boss at work or do not have a sense of achievement. Sometimes you are unmotivated because you're not hungry enough to see a desire come true. We all have the dreams of becoming something, but sometimes the motivation is not sufficient for us to get there.

One of my mentors used to tell me that no one can motivate anyone. Everyone is motivated by something. My idea of motivation may not be the same as yours. The person who chooses to sleep in is just as motivated as the person who strives to climb the corporate ladder. The one who chose to sleep in was motivated by his bed, while the person who wanted to be the next leader in the company was motivated by the success that he saw.

Sometimes we are motivated by our circumstances. Starting a business is not an easy path to take, but you must be motivated enough to work on the business because, if you don't, you might go hungry. Your 'wants' and 'needs' will sometimes motivate you to do certain things. Have a look at yourself and find out what motivates you.

- **Perfection**

There is no such thing as perfection. It is just another tool in the toolbox for procrastination. It's an excuse to not do anything for fear that it will not come out perfect.

I used to be like that. Unless I knew that I could do it and have a 100% success rate, I would not even bring myself to do it. I can recall a time when I was asked to master a language that I was not fluent in. Growing up, I was too proud to admit that I did not know that language well enough, although it was clear for everyone (and myself) to see. I went to a few classes, but it didn't go far enough, and I gave up on it. Not because I wasn't motivated or maybe because I was not motivated *enough*. I gave up because I wanted to be fluent from the first day. That was an impossible thing to do if you were learning a second language. I was also too proud to laugh at myself when I pronounced the words wrong or didn't know how to write them properly. Having other people make fun of me wasn't nice, to begin with. Now that I'm much older, I regret having that perfection mentality. To this day my Mandarin isn't the best. I can manage some conversation, but I am unable to read or write it. That said, I continue to work on my spoken Mandarin whenever the chance arises.

Taking charge of your success

The first thing you need to do to overcome the impediments to your success is to understand what is holding you back. Again, shift your mindset to think about what would happen if you did not have these impediments? What will it do to your life and to your business or career? Would you quit your job tomorrow to operate a food truck?

Here are a few steps that you can take to overcome impediments:

Irrevocable decision

Make yourself a promise. This promise is irrevocable, meaning that it cannot be reversed. It is one way, and you have to commit to it until the end. This is a promise or a covenant that you make with yourself. It's OK to start something imperfectly, but *start* something. Peter the disciple was the only other human that was said to have walked on water. But he had to take that first step of faith to get out of the boat. Do not give yourself an 'out'. Once you have arrived on the island and your intention is to take it over, burn the ship!

I have worked with many people who have stable jobs but have an innate desire to start something new or to work on a business. They may take that first step to starting a business by doing it part time or work on it in the evenings and weekends. Many of these businesses never really took off because the entrepreneurs continued to spend their most productive hours working for someone else, and their own dreams and desires took second place. Hear me out—there is nothing wrong with that. Some people deliberately choose to sell makeup or health drinks as a side business, or even participate in a gig-economy of some kind (rideshare or delivery driver). I am talking about people who have big audacious goals; who are working a dead-end job during the day so that they can continue to afford the things they had to commit to. If you don't fully immerse yourself in a cause, the chance that you'll succeed in building up that business is not very high. Take that irrevocable decision and, once you have a peace of mind about it, take the plunge. Bob Proctor, a guru in wealth-building, has this to say, "Jump off that building. You will grow wings on your way down". "What if I fail?", you might ask. Well, if you continue to dwell on all possible failures, then you are *likely* to fail.

For many of my clients, working with a coach is a big step. It is part of an irrevocable decision because it is an investment in their own future. Now that they have committed to working with someone they trust, they will begin to build on a roadmap of accountability – a blueprint of success – and continue to be responsible for taking on tasks that may seem uncomfortable but are essential for the success of their business.

High-leverage activities

Refer to the timetable that you completed in the previous chapter. How many of the tasks that you do are high-leverage activities? How much time do you spend on mundane, wasteful stuff that does not give you any results? Shift yourself to desire the results that you dream of and focus your attention on the activities that will get you to where you want to go.

It is also likely that when you start a business, a period of difficulty may present itself. You will have to grease your elbows and get down and dirty, to build the business and to build *on* the business at the same time. The result, though, is truly rewarding. Having worked with numerous entrepreneurs, even those that didn't make it to the big league, I've been told by all of them that they had no regrets about having started their own business, and it was one of the things they did that gave them the greatest joy.

In previous chapters, I have highlighted how you can start to look at the million and one things that are on your to-do list and begin to segment them to identify the activities that will get you nearer to your goals. Bad at accounting and bookkeeping? Hire a bookkeeper or accountant. No time to clean the house? Hire a cleaner. By leveraging other experts, you can continue to be the expert in your field.

Reflection

What do you believe is stopping you from taking action? Is it fear? Is it procrastination? Many times, we justify our actions when we do not perform or take charge of our successes. What excuse are you giving yourself to stop you from moving forward?

www.ingramcontent.com/pod-product-compliance
Lightning Source LLC
Chambersburg PA
CBHW072021110526
44592CB00012B/1396